Let Us Start with Africa

LET US START WITH AFRICA
FOUNDATIONS OF RASTAFARI SCHOLARSHIP

Edited by
Jahlani Niaah and Erin MacLeod

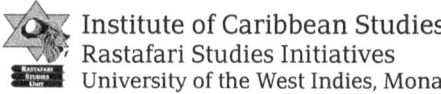

The University of the West Indies Press
Jamaica • Barbados • Trinidad and Tobago

Institute of Caribbean Studies
Rastafari Studies Initiatives
University of the West Indies, Mona

The University of the West Indies Press
7A Gibraltar Hall Road, Mona
Kingston 7, Jamaica
www.uwipress.com

© 2013 Jahlani Niaah and Erin MacLeod
All rights reserved. Published 2013

A catalogue record of this book is available from the National Library of Jamaica.

ISBN: 978-976-640-409-3

Cover illustration: Detail from *Emmanuel I* by Clinton Hutton (acrylic on paper, 2009).

Frontispiece: Bongo Joe (with flag) and an unidentified Nyahbinghi brethren at the opening ceremony of the Rastafari Studies Conference, the University of the West Indies, August 2010. Photo © Rastafarispeaks.com.

Book and cover design by Maria Papaefstathiou
maria.pap@graphicart-news.com

Illustrations by Michael Thompson
mikethompson5@mac.com

Printed in the United States of America.

Livicated to the memory of
Barry Chevannes,
Rex Nettleford,
Mortimo Planno
and Carole Yawney

Contents

Foreword
Rupert Lewis ix

Acknowledgements xi

Introduction
Jahlani Niaah and Erin MacLeod 1

1. From the Cross to the Throne
   Rex Nettleford 10

2. Polite Violence
   Mortimo Planno 22

3. You Must Be Willing to Reason Together
   Roy Augier 43

4. When Goldilocks Met the Dreadlocks
   Reflections on the Contributions of
   Carole D. Yawney to Rastafari Studies
   John Homiak 56

5. The Call of the Rastafari
   Barry Chevannes 117

Contributors 131

Foreword

Allow me to commend Jahlani Niaah and Erin MacLeod for putting together this collection which adds in significant ways to historicizing the growth, development and impact of Rastafari, and which also draws our attention to the developing field of Rastafari scholarship. This volume is historic because it marks the final words, so to speak, of the formidable Rastafari leader, Mortimo Planno, as well as the pioneering scholarship of Rex Nettleford, Barry Chevannes and Carole Yawney, who have made their transition.

The inaugural Rastafari Studies Conference (17–20 August 2010) held at the University of the West Indies, Mona, in Kingston, Jamaica, also marked a transition to a younger generation of Rastafari scholars, one of whom, Jahlani Niaah, was the conference's chief organizer. The late Barry Chevannes recognized this when at the end of the conference he called for a standing ovation for Niaah – his former student who had now become his teacher.

The conference saw a significant increase in the number of people who were investigating Rastafari in different disciplines within the academy, and among them were Rastafari scholars, male and female, with doctorates, who were insiders, studying and reflecting on the movement within the academy and sharing their work with the global academy and diverse Rastafari movements. The existence of global Rastafari communities is acknowledged in this volume, and their heterogeneity is expressed in the diverse nationalities as well as multi-racial and multi-linguistic features of a movement that was spawned in Jamaica in the 1930s.

The conference also marked the fiftieth anniversary of the 1960 publication *Report on the Rastafari Movement in Kingston, Jamaica*, and its only surviving author, Sir Roy Augier, provides the backstory to what is arguably the most important public policy report on the Rastafari movement on which basis several official missions to Africa were undertaken. The study arose from the request

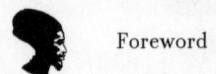 Foreword

of Mortimo Planno and other Rastafarians to Sir Arthur Lewis, then principal of the University College of the West Indies, who chose anthropologist M.G. Smith, historian Roy Augier and political theorist Rex Nettleford to undertake a survey of the Rastafari movement in Kingston. In addition to recommending the mission to African countries to arrange for the migration of Jamaicans to that continent, the report also recommended a wide-ranging set of social initiatives in Jamaica including the implementation of low-cost housing and the provision of social amenities such as electricity, water, sewage disposal and garbage collection and greater access to education for the Rastafari.

The central figure in this text is Mortimo Planno with his own reflective piece on "polite violence" which reminds us of the embattled lives not only in the British colonial era but also in the years after independence, and the extraordinary courage it took to proclaim Rastafari. In John Homiak's paper on Carole Yawney's work we get a picture of the fearlessness this white female Canadian of Ukrainian origin displayed in living and doing work in West Kingston, and becoming part of Planno's base in Trench Town. As a result of her ethnographic work we have a far greater understanding of Planno's modus operandi and his thinking as a pan-Africanist activist.

What is striking about this powerful collection is the range of perspectives that have been pulled together in discussing a movement in transition. The discussion on repatriation continues to stimulate debate about nationhood and about Jamaica as home, as evidenced in the comments of Sir Roy Augier and the late Barry Chevannes. Both enjoin Rastafari to see Jamaica as home. But in an era when the African Union hosts conferences to embrace the diaspora as the sixth region of the continent, the relationship between the Caribbean and Africa is being redefined to make possible more dynamic exchanges for development on both sides of the Atlantic and to continue the discussion around repatriation and reparations in keeping with the central pan-African themes developed by the Garvey movement and Rastafari throughout the twentieth century.

The presentations take us beyond the old conceptions of Rastafari as a millenarian movement, towards recognizing the movement as an epistemic foundation, a source of knowledge, of decolonizing philosophy and "livity" through collective reasoning and action.

Rupert Lewis
Professor of Political Thought
Department of Government
University of the West Indies, Mona

Acknowledgements

This book exists thanks to a number of people and institutions. Thanks to the University of the West Indies, Mona, for their continued support of Rastafari studies and hosting the inaugural Rastafari conference in 2010. As well, thanks to all who attended, asked questions, partook in conversations and continue to engage with Rastafari studies. Paul Thompson, Michele "Afifa" Harris, Lorna Smith and Rosina Casserly deserve thanks for transcribing and research assistance. We also extend gratitude to the CHASE Fund for help in archiving the work of Rastafari icon Mortimo Planno, and to Barry Chevannes and Joe Periera, as well as the Folk Filosofi support team of Mark "Nabbie Natural" Williams, Ira Embert, Cecil Gutzmore, Caroline Cooper, and Sonjah Stanley Niaah. The Office of the Principal at the Mona campus deserves credit and thanks for its continuous assistance. We are also grateful to the Radio Education Unit/Library of Spoken Word, University of the West Indies, Mona, for recording and archival assistance. Finally, the support of the Social Science and Humanities Research Council of Canada was also helpful in bringing this work to fruition.

Introduction
Jahlani Niaah and Erin MacLeod

The title of this collection provides us with a beginning. It is taken from Roy Augier's keynote lecture, collected herein, and the first lecture of the inaugural Rastafari Studies Conference held at the University of the West Indies (UWI), Mona, 17–20 August 2010. The four-day conference brought over ninety scholars and practitioners of Rastafari together to talk, listen and reason. Rastafari began, as Augier states, with Africa. From Garvey's prophetic call to look to the east, to the commitment of early adherents to a newly crowned king in Ethiopia, it is clear that Rastafari begins in Africa.

The Rastafari movement has been able to make the connection to Africa; this has been evident from the time of the earliest scholarship, which can be seen from the work of G.E. Simpson (1955) and Roger Mais (1954), and the subsequent work of Orlando Patterson (1964), Leonard Barrett (1968), Vera Rubin and Lambros Comitas (1976), and Sheila Kitzinger (1969). Each of these texts demonstrates Rastafari's ability to inspire and represent a discourse about Africa as being part and parcel of thinking deeply about Jamaican and Caribbean society, and in exposing the gaps that exist within that society. There is a disconnect that only becomes connected through the voice of Rastafari. What is the missing link? Seemingly, it is the location of Africa within the region's historical discourse.

In light of this, the date of this conference was not a coincidence. The year 2010 makes the connection with Africa, as it represents the eightieth anniversary of the coronation of His Imperial Majesty Haile Selassie in November of 1930. But it also marks the fiftieth anniversary of the landmark publication of the *Report on the Rastafari Movement in Kingston, Jamaica*, by scholars M.G. Smith, Roy Augier and Rex Nettleford. It is this report that played a singularly significant role in increasing our understanding of Rastafari. The report led to a mission to Africa, but it also was a publication that

Introduction

demonstrated the role of the academe in recognizing and supporting Rastafari. With the publication of this book, *Let Us Start With Africa: Honouring Rastafari Scholarship* – a text meant to both commemorate and celebrate scholars and practitioners of Rastafari – our aim is to demonstrate not only a range of thinking about the movement but the ways in which the movement, a movement which takes reasoning as a key practice, has encouraged reasoning about itself, the pan-African community and the international African presence.

This collection of papers takes into account the reach of Rastafari, and provides practitioners and scholars with previously unpublished material, much of it transcribed from lectures. Rex Nettleford and Mortimo Planno provide foundational thoughts for the volume. These papers were not presented at the UWI Rastafari conference, but they are invaluable for setting the stage for the three papers by Roy Augier, John Homiak and Barry Chevannes which were presented at the conference.

Coordination of the conference required attempts to bridge the worlds of various Rastafari communities, interests and expressions spanning landscapes and cyberspace, face to face interaction, and the all-important reasoning in a bid to engage key issues that have faced, and continue to face, Rastafari. It is always something of a tense undertaking for the "Powers" and "Principalities" – or the "official" society, as the University of the West Indies and the government of Jamaica are viewed – to facilitate dialogue between the Rastafari and the wider society. At the same time, the Rastafari movement has been one of the most consistent and accommodating towards the engagement of official society. And what has been the consistent topic of conversation? Their thinking on Africa. But Rastafari is also keenly interested in the world as well, and the world in Rastafari. From Ethiopia to Japan to New Zealand to Ghana to Brazil to Canada to the United Kingdom and Jamaica, the global development and globalization of Rastafari is evident. We hope that the pieces herein will resonate with all of these different groups and groupings of Rastafari.

The conference itself gave way to different discussions, some about the spiritual and mystical elements of Rastafari, others about practical and pragmatic issues concerning reparations as well as repatriation. During panel discussions, presentations were given and questions asked, but many important conversations were had in the in-between spaces – before panels, at lunch, in the evening. There were films, there was drumming, there was talking, there was chanting. There were elders, there were youth, there were women, there were men – there were many different peoples dealing with many different ideas, all in their own ways. Rastafari's multiplicity and acceptance of variety meant that all of these ways were evident at the conference. In this collection, we have attempted to reflect this variety and give voice to a number of pertinent and historically significant approaches and ideas that deal with a wide range of issues.

But it is not simply the commemoration of the conference that we wish to present in this volume. The conference did in 2010 what the report did in 1960: it connected Rastafari and the academy. It provided us with an opportunity to increase the critical representation of Rastafari in the literature, especially from indigenous and practitioner scholars. Collections such as *Chanting Down Babylon* (1998), *Rastafari: A Universal Philosophy in the Third Millennium* (2006) and *Rastafari in the New Millennium* (2012) have made attempts to provide kaleidoscopic portraits of the Rastafari experience and philosophy. Though these texts provide analysis and investigation, this anthology offers works of great introspection by individuals who each possess more than thirty years of engagement with the movement. Never before have their works been presented together in one volume. This collection offers retrospective analysis that will provide an essential expansion of Rastafari scholarship.

These papers illustrate the maturation of the field itself. It is now accepted that Rastafari does not fit into a paradigm. It is its own paradigm. The volume therefore represents an engagement with the paradigm that is Rastafari. In its presentation it demonstrates an elevated dialogue about the movement. Whereas more than half a century ago the academy entered Dungle, this volume represents the reverse voyage. It does not just talk about solutions, but also develops insights into problems and recognizes different perspectives. Some ideas may conflict with others and readers may have ideas of their own. All of this is encouraged by the authors represented here. As Paulo Friere has written, if we are truly interested in liberation, "action and reflection cannot proceed without the action and reflection of others" (1970, 126).

To understand how a connection between the academic world and that of Rastafari could occur requires looking back and listening to the voices that helped to maintain the link. In this interest, the collection begins with a 1999 keynote speech from Rex Nettleford at a Rastafari conference in honour of folk philosophy (or "folk filosofi"), entitled "From the Cross to the Throne" and held at the University of the West Indies. It was transcribed from

Introduction

the recording at that conference chaired by Mortimo Planno who provided an impromptu introduction of Nettleford. Nettleford uses the opportunity to place on the record the background for what became the Rastafari report, the technical mission to Africa and his overall assessment of, and regard for, the Rastafari movement as it has developed over the years since he first did his research. Not only does this piece provide interesting sociological insights into the conditions of the brethren at the time in Kingston, it also provides a framework to the historical linkages that the Rastafari engineered with the University of the West Indies and puts into perspective the wider value of the movement's national and regional pedagogy. Nettleford argues that the discourse of Rastafari was cardinal in shaping and directing important but omitted aspects of the fledgling independent country's intellectual engagement with a postcolonial dialogue and process. Nettleford was, by some accounts, the Rastafari's highest placed advocate, consistently drawing reference to Rastafari as a national achievement – a quantum leap even for Africans in the West – and recognizing, also, the way in which the movement aided scholars' realizations about Jamaican society, as well as themselves, and the core connection that the populace longed for, that is, the engagement with the African Presence (emphasizing that this is African Presence with a capital "P").

Nettleford's tenure as vice chancellor of the University of the West Indies from 1998 to 2004 was a fitting parallel for the journey and the achievement of the African Jamaican, particularly in the context of what he, Nettleford, elsewhere refers to as "smadification" – or the process of becoming someone of respectability, especially within the post-independence reconstruction period. Though Nettleford focuses on the victory of Rastafari in providing a corpus of ideas and attitudes which ensured that corrective measures were embraced by a society which had been long led away from its true identity, he also recognizes that this national agenda of Rastafari was a central thread for humanity in general. The address demonstrates the strength of Nettleford's powers of oration, even when he was thinking on his feet, and also the way in which the research that he took part in, in 1960, had remained deeply embedded in his lifework. Nettleford was, as a young scholar, part of the awakening of an interest in research on indigenous and even demeaned aspects of the Caribbean culture and personage. Not only was he one of the most engaged Jamaican scholars involved in representing and facilitating Rastafari expatiation, he was also at the forefront of the multimedia application of the movement's contribution, as can be seen through his

Introduction

creative works involving the music, lyrics, paintings, philosophies and opinions of the Rastafari. Indeed he was one of the movement's key apologists.

The second piece, "Polite Violence", one of Planno's lectures, given on the occasion of Mortimo Planno's first public lecture as a visiting fellow in folk philosophy in November 1998 at the University of the West Indies, provides a stark picture of the Babylon that has oppressed not just Rastafari but all of Jamaica, from colonialism to this day. As a teacher of Africa, Planno was able to transcend the humble environment of the inner-city community Dungle and the shanties of Kingston to, at the end of his active years, share his wisdom with students at the University of the West Indies. Planno is a classic representation of the way the Rastafari have evolved within the Jamaican society and, by virtue of their contribution, have demanded respect from the society. Planno's investment in the ideas of African liberation earned him the title of visiting professor at the University of the West Indies. This, no doubt, also had been greatly facilitated by Nettleford, in his position as vice chancellor, for he aimed to preserve the ideas of Planno, who had come to be recognized as a leading thinker within the Rastafari community.

Indeed, it was Planno who had the idea that the Rastafari movement should collectively approach the University of the West Indies. It was he who wrote the letter in 1960 asking for mediation between the Rastafari and the wider society, a society which, he argued, did not want Rastafari to have the rights and freedom expressed within the faith. "Polite Violence" was not the first of Planno's lectures – he had initially been asked to give a talk in 1997 in honour of Bob Marley. In his oral works, Planno offers not only a refreshing alternative perspective, but also invaluable information being both an adherent and a scholar of the movement. The invitation to speak at the university subsequently initiated a process of thinking and research at the

Introduction

university that saw the introduction of a programme described as folk philosophy (or *folk filosofi*). This programme hosted a range of contributors (including Robin "Jerry" Small and Mutabaruka), welcoming them on campus to interact with students and faculty, and inviting them to become involved in teaching and research at this level. Planno himself was provided with a residential fellowship from 1998 until his death in 2006. Planno opened the door which allowed the Rastafari and the university scholars and students to engage in dialogue with the wider society. He was also instrumental in the establishment of the Rastafari studies agenda at the university, having articulated the need for a "new faculty of interpretation".

Roy Augier stands as the only surviving author of the 1960 report to have witnessed the inaugural Rastafari Studies Conference. As a St Lucian, Augier brings a pan-Caribbean perspective to the pan-African ideals of Rastafari. His support of Rastafari, as an academic, has led him to recognize the need to lobby for the dissemination of Caribbean and African histories that address the experiences of an Afro-Caribbean society. The need to understand both the African experience and Rastafari, rather than to oppress the movement, was evident to Augier, Nettleford and Smith. As the speaker who opened the Rastafari conference with a lecture anthologized herein, Augier stands sympathetic to the Rastafari movement as well as critical of it. His lecture, the first published commentary he has provided on the movement since the report, raised the curtain on the conference along with many questions – as well as eyebrows.

Augier describes the need for a strong relationship between the Caribbean and Africa. However, whereas many Rastafari call for a direct connection and repatriation to Africa, Augier, thinking back over fifty years, presents a trajectory that leads not physically but spiritually to Africa within the Caribbean in general and specifically in Jamaica. Given the Rastafari focus on repatriation to Africa, specifically Ethiopia, this wish to find Africa in Jamaica was met with jeers.

What Augier did was present his own argument for an understanding of Africa's history as well as its contemporary existence. Augier then called for investment in the homeland, that is Jamaica. Though his lecture received a standing ovation, his perspective was the source of much post-conference controversy. Ras Marcus, a commenter on the Rastafari Speaks website (www.rastafarispeaks.com), referred to the lecture as "sad and outrageous, and a form of brain washing". Augier knew he was challenging the fundamental Rastafari tenet of repatriation as a physical movement, and he was given immediate feedback while speaking and then further feedback following the conference. His presentation of such a speech and the response to it demonstrates not only that critique is an inherent part of the movement, but also lays bare the accompanying reality of the reasoning process. As a scholar of Rastafari and as a Caribbean intellectual, he provides an example of the breadth of thinking that exists as regards negotiating the African presence – that being the theme of the conference itself and a foundation of Rastafari thinking.

John Homiak's piece also provides insight into the negotiation of the African presence in Jamaica, but from the perspective of an anthropologist. Like all other pieces in this collection, his essay began as an oral presentation. He has expanded the presentation, however, specially for this volume, tackling the history of research on Rastafari and providing insight into the methodology and approach of Carole Yawney. Homiak's essay describes the late scholar's ground-breaking ethnographic work, which led to a more nuanced understanding of Rastafari. Yawney's championing of Mortimo Planno, and her dogged thirty-year documentation of his speeches and lectures have created a trove of invaluable artefacts. As a student of the veritable university he held in Trench Town at his 18 Fifth Street address, she has provided perhaps the most important record of Planno's methodology and praxis through her long relationship with him and his circle. Homiak describes the ways in which Yawney's research was transformative, both for herself and the movement, as her advocacy and activism helped to spread information about Rastafari beyond Jamaica.

However, Homiak's piece presents more than just a history of Yawney's life's work; it is a fitting tribute to a passionate scholar of Rastafari. The essay also puts into perspective the ways in which her research on Rastafari had been achieved. Yawney, according to Homiak, was able to fine-tune her research methodology and develop her critical insights – not just about Rastafari, but about anthropological investigation in general. Homiak describes Yawney's enthnographic work and explains how she adapted the methodology to research and analyse Rastafari, and Planno in particular.

Anthropologist Vered Amit writes, "The answer to what happens to anthropology if its practitioners adapt their fieldwork practices to the exigencies of new circumstances is that it wouldn't remain as anthropology if they didn't" (2000, 17). As Homiak demonstrates, Yawney was keenly aware of the circumstances that gave birth to and developed the Rastafari movement, and she adapted her approach to these circumstances. Her work thus

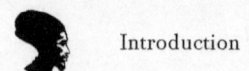

Introduction

illustrates the development of an anthropological practitioner as well as the development of practices to consider when researching Rastafari as an outsider. Yawney focused on all this while consistently recognizing, reverently, as she did, the importance of Rastafari, commenting that "the opportunity to move amongst Rastafari is a privilege that cannot be taken for granted" (1999, 154).

The final piece is that by the late Barry Chevannes, a lecture that ended the conference. Chevannes was the most prolific Jamaican scholar of Rastafari, and what is presented here is his last major contribution to the field, sealing his forty years of engagement with the movement. Chevannes was at the helm of the Faculty of the Social Sciences in the late 1990s and was responsible for inviting Planno to speak as well as establishing the importance of folk philosophy at the University of the West Indies. His earlier work in anthropology had set the stage for his intellectual and national engagement with African Caribbean religions and culture. For him, *folk filosofi* was a natural progression as the Caribbean came of age and indigenous scholarship became more recognized.

To this extent Chevannes embraced the core pedagogical philosophy of Rastafari which advocated equality and equity, as far as knowledge was concerned, by insisting that "each one, teach one". He thus deliberately sought to immerse students in the oft taken for granted sources that existed in the world around them. Folk philosophy thus had a natural place in the academy, as it was argued by Chevannes to be responsible for who we are as a people. In his lecture at the Rastafari conference, he presented a means of moving forward, while still remaining grounded in the past experiences of Rastafari practice and scholarship. Chevannes also asks us to "start with Africa" when beginning with Rastafari and appreciate the values of the movement, advising young and more experienced scholars to account for that which has come before.

Nettleford, Planno, Augier, Homiak, Yawney and Chevannes form a core foundation of scholars and thinkers who have engaged in research seeking to mediate between the under-represented and devalued elements of African culture and the scholarly representation of these traditions. Nettleford would later advance the idea of the need to make visible the submerged African Presence. He would eventually come to assert that even the very space which one was occupying and how one carried oneself was also reclamation of Africa. Nettleford and his contemporaries bring the clarity that the Rastafari movement advanced the debate about the invisibility of the African element – not least of which was the invisibility of the teaching of Africa or the Caribbean in any fundamental way.

In each piece in this volume, however, Africa is visible and vivid. The collection provides a varied selection of commentary and ideas on Rastafari – some in conversation, some contradictory. It is therefore important to recall the discursive nature of Rastafari, a movement that respects discussion and dialogue. As the Rastafari movement and its accompanying scholarship continue, and show no signs of abatement, it is perhaps fitting to end the way Augier ended his lecture. Given the wide variety of perspectives that Rastafari allows, we, as Augier urged, must be willing to reason together.

To the next fifty years of Rastafari and Rastafari scholarship.

References

Amit, Vered. 2000. *Constructing the Field: Ethnographic Fieldwork in the Contemporary World.* London: Routledge.

Barnett, Michael, ed. 2012. *Rastafari in the New Millennium: A Reader.* Syracuse, NY: Syracuse University Press.

Barrett, Leonard. 1968. *The Rastafarians*. Boston: Beacon Press.

Friere, Paulo. 1970. *Pedagogy of the Oppressed*. New York: Continuum.

Kitzinger, Sheila. 1969. "Protest and Mysticism: The Ras Tafari Cult in Jamaica". *Journal for the Scientific Study of Religion* 8:240–62.

Mais, Roger. 1954 (2007). *Brotherman*. New York: Macmillan.

Murell, N. Samuel, William David Spencer and Adrian A. McFarlane. 1998. *Chanting Down Babylon: The Rastafari Reader*. Philadelphia: Temple University Press.

Patterson, Orlando. 1964. "Ras Tafari: Cult of Outcasts". *New Society* 4 (3): 15–17.

Rubin, Vera and Lambros Comitas. 1976. *Ganja in Jamaica: The Effects of Marijuana Use*. New York: Doubleday.

Simpson, G.E. 1955. "Political Cultism in West Kingston, Jamaica". *Social and Economic Studies* 4 (2): 133–49.

Smith, M.G., Roy Augier, Rex Nettleford. 1960. *Report on the Rastafari Movement in Kingston, Jamaica*. Kingston: Institute of Social and Economic Studies.

Yawney, Carole. 1999. "Only Visitors Here: Representing Rastafari into the 21st Century". In *Religion, Diaspora, and Cultural Identity,* edited by John Pulis. Amsterdam: Gordon and Breach.

Zips, Werner. 2006. *Rastafari: A Universal Philosophy in the Third Millennium*. Kingston: Ian Randle.

Chapter 1

From the Cross to the Throne

Rex Nettleford

Introduction by Ras Mortimo "Kumi" Planno[1]

Tenayistellen![2] Greetings!

Our vice chancellor is here to bring us up to date on certain things about this year [i.e., 1999 and the anticipations about the turn of the millennium] – you know globalization [the] year of consciousness [and commensurate global consciousness of this twenty-first century]. Now the first thing I should say is thanks to the University of the West Indies people, including Professor Nettleford, when the UCWI [University College of the West Indies] presented that report you have people with the audacity to say, "It is unworthy to scholars." Independent minded people who recognized people and who love people too.

So I going ask Professor Nettleford to give us a page in the history . . . of this thing.

We came to the university extra-mural department.[3] We had written [a] letter to Dr Lewis;[4] Dr Lewis suggested that we should contact the extra-mural department, although we had already written to them. Anyhow, to cut a long story short . . . we go to where the recommendation of the principality and powers – the university had made a recommendation that they should deal with this back to Africa thing.

You know the Rastaman primary interest [is] in repatriation. [In t]he report, . . . the principal made some recommendation to government that a mission should be sent to Africa, a "fact-finding" [mission]. The fact-finding mission was sent to Africa, and I was allowed to go on the first fact-finding mission. This is in April 1961, and when we came back in June after spending nine weeks in Africa, we mek a recommendation report and the government of the day sey, well they will send a follow-up by sending an official mission which our vice chancellor Professor Nettleford was leader of . . . Aston Foreman and Clarke[5] was on it too. Well, when Dr Nettleford came back – them bring back a report – supposed to be treated as how they have treated the minority report [which is] what they called our report, when we came back 1961 [in] June. So what they did then was shelve that report and government was put out of power, and is what now, thirty-nine years?

One of the media people ask me, "Den why oono a go waste money pon Rastaman argument and ting?", but this is a page of history and those of you who have children who coming to Rasta and ask them question concerning CXC examination[6] and other exams and asking bout the history of it will learn it an learn the truth of it: where it started and where it is going and where it reach. Now I got the opportunity to look upon the week affairs [10 August 1999 to 15 August 1999[7]]. International affairs in the world, world affairs – the last eclipse of the sun – and we have a discussion period between old Rastaman and young Rastaman who don't have the experience of world affairs and things.[8] So we [not] going waste much time now – beg you hear from professor, vice chancellor, Nettleford what was the report that he brought back from Africa in his official mission – and what happened – for a lot of us – young Rasta, old Rasta – don't know nothing to add to that part of the history we are part of. So without further ado – I ask brother, professor, vice chancellor, and call him what you may – my brother Nettleford, I would ask you to explain to us about what happen to your report that you brought weh we don't hear fi thirty-nine years.

We will still listen it.

Brother, elder patriarch, ancestral icon – Planno – my colleague Professor Chevannes, dean of the Faculty [of Social Science], I didn't quite come to be put on the spot. Knowing Brother Planno, though, I should have been prepared for that. Actually that "report" was never published. In fact, we had been summoned back prematurely from the four-month tour that we were on in Africa because the Jamaican election had to be called. The government of the day lost the elections, and [at the time] the "report" was shelved;

Rex Nettleford

I am not even sure it was read. Following that, the rest is not quite history – some things happened. The succeeding government did something else which interested many of us: they decided that if Mohammed could not go to the mountain, they would bring the mountain to Mohammed. So it arrived in 1966 – and we remember that fantastic day; he [Emperor Haile Selssie] was imprisoned with love in the war and it was Brother Planno who had to get him out.[9] The Ethiopians were very interested in the [Rastafari] movement, contrary to what was being said in Jamaica about it all being nonsense. I remember when we had an audience with the emperor.[10] Of course he spoke to us with a translator in Amharic. At one point, the translator had to leave the room, and in his absence the emperor said to us in perfect English, "How are my people?" Some time after Emperor Selassie's visit, we went down to Shashamane – brothers and sisters know what that place is – a bit of land in Ethiopia that his majesty had given to blacks from the Western world. It was very interesting – it was obvious that the only people who could go and break the back of that land were true believers and I think his majesty understood this. So we came back with a firm realization that a number of persons from here could go to settle in Ethiopia. There was of course at the time a very strong movement of Islam into parts of Africa – Ethiopia included; and we know the ancestral pedigree of the Ethiopian Orthodox Church – the centre for the Coptic religion having been moved years ago from Alexandria to Addis Ababa. Therefore, it was felt that people like the Rastafarians would indeed bring back some balance there. So we were taken seriously on several grounds. I have no doubt that the energy, commitment, dedication and faith of the Rastafarian could have made a difference in that vast expanse of land around Shashamane as was intended.

Even more important is what the movement has meant to Jamaica in particular, and to the Caribbean and the African diaspora throughout the world in general. This contribution is greatly underestimated – taken for granted by many of us in Jamaica unfortunately – but a good thing can't be killed. And although the Rastafarian movement may at times appear to be muted, the fact is that it has been a great catalyst in changing the perception of social reality in the Western world. The African Presence – capital "A", capital "P" – itself has been underestimated by our own scholars and by others generally. From time immemorial, that African Presence has been a positive and very strong determinant of human civilization. The grief and ruin which Europe likes to regard as its own cradles of civilization were in fact crossroad civilizations in which the Africans played a very important role; interestingly, if you go to Egypt – which the Ethiopians once ruled – you will find that all the colonizers who went in, came out Egyptianized rather than the other way around. This is the effect of Africa. This can be seen again later in history, in the Iberian peninsula which was responsible for much of what happed in this part of the world from 1492 onwards and which gave rise to many of us being here. It, too, was another crossroad civilization consisting of Moors, Jews, Iberians and Europeans who in fact produced for the world great art, science, architecture and literature. This civilization was heavily influenced by the North African presence, which gave it form and purpose. Over the past five hundred years, the African diaspora has also been central to the formation of the Americas, and here I do not merely refer to the United States.[11]

Mortimo Planno

Now, how much should the government have to do with the Rastafarians? A great deal, because out of all the people who have been fighting for the dignity and the justice of people of African ancestry, it is the Rastafarians who have made the kind of quantum leap that all civilizations must make, in terms of determining their own God, their own image. This is a fantastic development which is not usually understood. When we wrote that report in 1960, we were regarded as blasphemous. The *Gleaner* wrote an editorial which was damning and those at the University of the West Indies spoke disparagingly about those wild, unruly, silly people.[12] They have lived to eat their words, thank God, but still this kind of criticism is what we were subjected to.

That 1960 report was very important, and I would like to take this opportunity to welcome the Rastafari movement back home to the university. I remember when I was just back from school [in the United Kingdom] as a young man and working at [the University of the West Indies], I thought I could solve every problem in the world. I was very critical of Jamaican society, as I still am in a certain regard. I would voice my opinion on the radio, and some of the Rastafari brothers probably heard me and would come to my office to talk to me. My office was just across there, in the extra-mural department where I

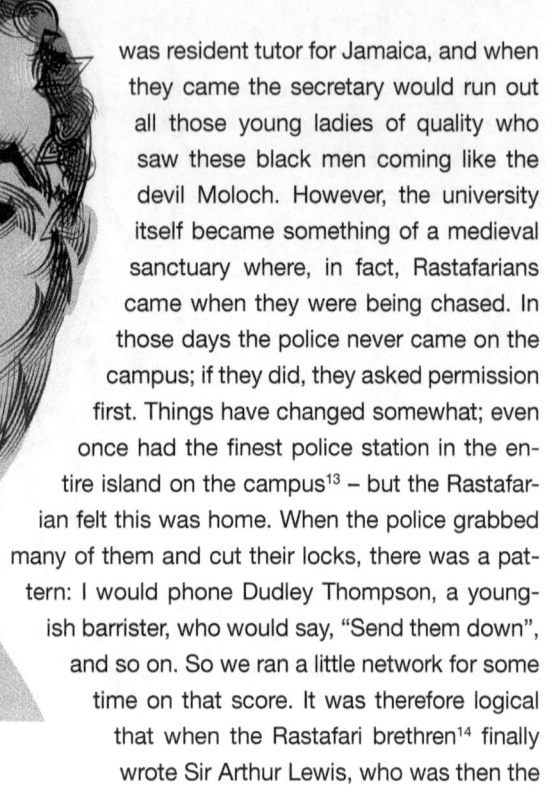
Marcus Garvey

was resident tutor for Jamaica, and when they came the secretary would run out all those young ladies of quality who saw these black men coming like the devil Moloch. However, the university itself became something of a medieval sanctuary where, in fact, Rastafarians came when they were being chased. In those days the police never came on the campus; if they did, they asked permission first. Things have changed somewhat; even once had the finest police station in the entire island on the campus[13] – but the Rastafarian felt this was home. When the police grabbed many of them and cut their locks, there was a pattern: I would phone Dudley Thompson, a youngish barrister, who would say, "Send them down", and so on. So we ran a little network for some time on that score. It was therefore logical that when the Rastafari brethren[14] finally wrote Sir Arthur Lewis, who was then the principal of the university, they would speak of me, requesting that I take part in the preparation of the 1960 report. That is how I, Professor Augier, a historian, and M.G. Smith, who had been working a good deal on social conditions in Kingston, got together.

So we started our survey. I used to be in Dungle,[15] which was later stabilized into what is now called Tivoli Gardens, and Back-o-Wall until 2 a.m. without any fear of being shot or what have you. I would drive Arthur Lewis around at 1 a.m., going to the brethren meetings then. I remember having long talks with Prince Emmanuel,[16] who was still living there before moving out to St Thomas, Sam Brown[17] and Brother Planno, of course, who, even then, was very assertive and understood where the movement should go, and what it was all about. We learnt a great deal.

One of the things that I found was most and who were sort of leaders were people of my age at the time – in mid-twenties and I found that all of them were bright – very bright – and what had really happened to many of them was that when the bandwagon started to roll after the war [World War II] in education – there just wasn't enough space to take in all the people who really ought to have been on that and that indeed forced many of them into really saying what this society was about.[18] Here you had a sizeable number of people being forced to function as a cultural minority in their own country. This of course propelled them to reflect upon their society and to create a paradigm which would make sense for them. I was very impressed by that. I shared this with Sir Arthur on our long trips in and out of the university. He said to me once, and I have always remembered it, "We are all Rastas." I understood that for obvious reasons, if only because of the way I look – bald head or not. It was only later that I discovered that his father was a Garveyite in St Lucia, and had taken him to a UNIA [Universal Negro Improvement Association] meeting when he was nine years old. Sir Arthur never forgot that, and that is what inspired him to really think seriously about how societies like our own have been structured. The Rastafarian report, of which we printed ten thousand, sold off in two hours. Mind you, it was six pence a copy, but six pence was a lot of money in those days. We learnt from that endeavour how we could inform public policy with our research and writing.

Mr Norman Manley[19] was a man who was greatly underrated. I remember, as a youngster, having long talks with him about the movement and he said here we were seeing a pimple on a sick land, a sick body politic. [Rastafari and Back to Africa are] in the bloodstream and we had to do something about it. His advisors at the time cautioned him against [engaging with the movement at all]. They felt [the Rastafari movement] was nonsense – they believed this was a cult which shouldn't be taken seriously. [Norman Manley] didn't pay any attention to them; he came to the university because we felt for one thing that a mission should be sent [to Africa], and seriously constituted involving members of the movement to go and see for themselves and it was followed up by the technical mission of which I was a member, as Brother Planno says. So the university learnt a great deal from this interface between town and gown, which, happily, the Faculty of Social Sciences, led by Dean Chevannes, insists on maintaining, as it allows us to discover the new and appropriate bodies of knowledge which will take us into the twenty-first century.

As a result of that 1960 report, a number of things happened. There is now a rich body of literature on the Rastafarians and indeed a lot of interest in the movement from people all over the world. I have had many letters from young Africans in east, west and south Africa who want to know more about this Rastafarian movement. The influence has been very strong, and this is reflected especially in the music. I keep telling people that the music, from ska right through to reggae and I presume dancehall, appropriated the Rastafarian movement not the other way around. People don't understand this. In fact reggae has taken to itself an ontology, a way of being; a cosmology, a way of thinking about the world; and an epistemology, a way of knowing. The Rastafarian movement doesn't usually get credit for it. Mr Marley, as we know, decided that he had to employ not only the outward signs but also the inward grace of the movement. There are some other entertainers who do not sport locks, but their inner landscape is very much dependent on the tenets of the Rastafarian movement, the movement which held a mirror up to Jamaica and said to it, "Look in the mirror, what do you see – Snow White?" Some people actually said yes, but I think many others decided that they had better come to terms with reality. The other thing is that the movement provided a wonderful landing pad for many of the people above Torrington Bridge who were in the search for self; so middle-class parents had to come to terms with the migrations of their sons and daughters into the movement. I choreographed a dance dealing with this kind of issue in 1964, called "Two Drums for Babylon".[20] In it are two brown characters – a lady of quality and her fiancé. On the eve of their wedding, the fellow finds the Rastafari faith, and she goes into the camp after him only to end up with the Rasta chief. Lots of people thought that was blasphemous and quite out of order.

The influence of the movement has been far reaching and deeply penetrating. Rastafarians must take every credit for this, because they really have been forcing people in Jamaica to accept the fact that they are black. I have never seen a blacker country which is afraid of blackness. One of the marvellous things about Rastafarians, and one of the things which I draw upon to strengthen my own resolve to be a better person, is that they are race conscious without being racist. It is a delicate balance of sensibility which I first found among the Rastafarians; that is the inheritance which now informs the entire music industry and the movement – all those fellows writing conscious lyrics. The other aspect of this particular sensibility is that there is hope in despair. Oh yes, we give the country hell, yet though we say things are bad, there is always a thread of hope. This hope in despair is something that keeps us going, and we owe it to the Rastafarians to keep going.

Lastly, the more things change the more they remain the same. So the struggle continues, but we have to stay in there, stay the course. I read an article in the *Gleaner*[21] by a lady journalist who has a thing about people like us. She was going on about patois today, condemning it as terrible. She says that it is a language because people speak it, but it is not capable of conveying abstract thought. To this I say, what then of the Rastas and our people who pass on to us some of the most profound proverbs through their story telling, through their wit? Patois is able to take the most complex of ideas and condense it into two lines. You know, I am in a job[22] which is very interesting; the title sounds good, but it is something of a stress. Many people ask me, "How are you doing?" "How is it?" There is only one way I can genuinely describe it, whether I read Kant, Wittgenstein, Plato or Aristotle. The answer is, "More water than flour", and I can't state it any better or more profoundly than that. Because, the truth of the matter is that there are people in positions of trust, who have the attention of our population, who still write this nonsense that the kind of language – the kind the ordinary people of Jamaica speak – the kind of "I" words invented by the Rastafarian, the kind of expressions that are used by people who are seriously thinking about the society, is not capable of philosophical expression. That kind of snobbery relegates us to being bearers of wood and drawers of water because we can't think. And some of the most succinct thinking about this society and the African diaspora has been done by the Rastafarian movement.

On behalf of the university I want to thank you for this, because this is a definite contribution to the advancement and the building of knowledge. So, thank you. Africa, in a funny kind of way, is where you are, is your sphere where you walk, and even the amount of space you take up in holding that head high rather than low. That's Africa. Don't worry about people saying that its myth and legend; don't worry about this notion that you ought to have a hermeneutics and exegesis – don't even try to understand the words. The point is, there is a kind of inner logic and inner consistency in a movement which you have built, which must itself undergo changes as all great religions and all great movements have had to do. At the same time it must hold on to the core which is rooted strongly in human dignity, in the rehumanization of people of African ancestries after five hundred years of obscenities. As I was saying just now to a colleague, I have long decided that among the things that I would never recommend to any people is slavery, and we have every right to keep fighting it and not forget what it has done.

[On the question of repatriation:[23]]
The matter of repatriation is still in the cards. The struggle continues and it has to be yours, so keep at it. One of the things we found – especially when we did that thing [reference to the 1960–62 efforts by way of fact finding missions] thirty years ago – was that repatriation is predicated on the willingness of the receiving countries to have us back. This is very important and it was

what struck us within Ethiopia at the time. I am not sure where the authorities in Ethiopia stand now and maybe we really should take another exploratory trip to find out. That is the most I could say. But repatriation is one of the cornerstones of the Rastafarian movement. I find the level of sophistication is great – the Christians say the kingdom of heaven is within you – not up in the clouds where there are lots of bees and cows.[24] We found among the brothers and sisters that [for this] inner landscape you have to be very sure yourself. What I have found is that there has been an Africanization of the consciousness of Jamaicans, thanks to the Rastafarian; many Rastafarians understood that as one form of expression of repatriation. There are many people who are living here, but whose minds are elsewhere. Marcus Garvey, incidentally, was thinking along exactly the same lines that you are now thinking, when he said, "Emancipate yourself from mental slavery":[25] he too believed that repatriation had to be on several levels.

[On the matter of the contribution of Rastafari to the Africanization of consciousness:]
One of the things not clearly written up is the tremendous influence which the Rastafari movement has. When I say the "Africanization of consciousness", it is this influence that I am talking about. This [Africanization of consciousness] is what should have happened in 1962, [but] somebody declared that we were with the west and we know what that means – nothing [by way of raising African consciousness] happened between 1962 and the Rodney Riots.[26] Nothing really happened, in terms of propelling this country forward. It is why I am so worried that we are spending so much time talking about bleaching and chicken pills – this is a mentality that goes way back, it is a mentality we should have left behind a long time ago. So there is the role still for the Rastafarian. Ideas are fragile, and people will adopt them for some time and then abandon them. The next thing you know is that they are broken; there are always forces in a society like this, which is deeply Eurocentric, that result in the denegation of things African. The Caribbean, with the Rastafari movement, is a dynamic laboratory which has really been trying to work out the role of Africa in the human development and in fact preparing many people for the twenty-first century.

So, let not your heart be troubled – neither let it be afraid; we are working on that right knowledge. I must tell you the restoration of Emancipation Day is very interesting. I happen to have chaired the committee which recommended it; it is something which I felt very strongly about. I grew up as an emancipation baby. But I discovered some very interesting things about our people when we went around the country asking people what they think [about reinstating Emancipation Day] – most people were in favour of it. But I got from some quarters including many teachers the notion that emancipation has nothing to do with us because we were not the only people who were enslaved. You get that kind of nonsense, but happily everybody decided it had to be reinstated. You will be happy to know that everybody [is reinstating Emancipation Day] – Trinidad – reinstated 1983 – Barbados, Virgin Islands, Netherland Antilles, through our work in [UNESCO] – transatlantic slavery is a crime against humanity.

I would not have been able to have understand all of these things had it not been for my new connection in Jamaica and that reality has been greatly underpinned by the Rastafarian movement.

Acknowledgements

This talk was given by Rex Nettleford at the Rastafari conference and assembly "From the Cross to the Throne", University of the West Indies, Mona, 15 August 1999.

Notes

1. Planno, in this introduction, speaks in a combination of standard English and patois (or patwa). The transcription has been edited for clarity. Further, his discourse style is what ethnographer Carole Yawney describes as being driven by synchronicity, so throughtout his conversation he pulls on incidents and activities which converge within specific time and space.
2. This is a transliteration of a common Amharic greeting.
3. The University College of the West Indies – UCWI, as it was first called when it was established in 1948 as a college of London University – created an extra-mural department within the university to provide the Caribbean community with essential outreach services. This was seen as an integral part of the very concept of being a regional university.
4. This is a reference to Sir William Arthur Lewis, a St Lucian economist, the first Afro-Caribbean national to head the university.

5. The second mission to Africa being referred to here was called the "Technical Mission to Africa" which visited Nigeria, Ghana and Ethiopia. Along with Rex Nettleford, there was Aston Foreman, Don Mills and Wesley Miller. Planno's reference to "Clarke" is not clear.
6. Caribbean Examination Council, a regional body established in 1972 to replace the need for testing students in the region through the overseas exams originating from the United Kingdom.
7. On 11 August 1999 there was a highly scrutinized eclipse of the sun, the last of the millennium and considered to be one of the most highly viewed in human history.
8. Here Planno alludes to the fact that this is the character of the Rastafari to take interest in discussing all these things – the last eclipse of the sun before the millennium etc.
9. This bringing of the mountain to Mohammed refers to the invitation extended by the Jamaican government to Emperor Haile Selassie to visit the country. On his arrival at the airport, his plane was surrounded by a huge crowd and Planno was responsible for calming the crowd down and escorting the emperor off the plane.
10. Nettleford here refers to his trip to five African states including Ethiopia where he had audience with the Emperor in January to March 1962 as a part of a Government of Jamaica technical mission. See Augier and Salter (2010) for an account of this mission.
11. Nettleford remarked in his address, "The United States has managed to hijack the word America and claim it for its own designation, and we keep referring to citizens of the United States as Americans, when in fact the lands of the Western Hemisphere were originally known as the Americas."
12. Meaning the Rastafari.
13. Nettleford here laments about the overall changes in the society which have also affected the university where one of the best police posts was once upon a time – a place which was literally a sanctuary for the brethren where the police would not molest them.
14. Nettleford remarked that at that time there were not many sistren among the brethren in West Kingston where the survey of Rastafari was conducted by Smith, Nettleford and Augier. What we discovered was that the sistren were busily working while the brethren were taking care of the children – fathering.
15. At the time of the survey done by Nettleford et al., there was significant squatting in western Kingston, and the Rastafari inhabited much of these areas. The chief squatter communities were Dungle, Back-o-Wall and Ackee Walk. Additionally, members of the movement squatted in shanties along the shore of the Marcus Garvey Drive.

16. Prince Emmanuel (later, King Emmanuel) was one of the significant leaders to have emerged after the death of Leonard Howell, the founder of the movement. He was responsible for the formation of the Ethiopia Africa Black International Congress in 1958 and was also a part of the representation to the university which resulted in the report.
17. Sam Brown was yet another significant leader who along with Prince Emmanuel and Planno were apart of the leadership of the urban Rastafari sect in the 1950s and 1960s. Sam Brown had the further distinction of being the first Rastafari to contest the national elections in the early 1960s gaining fewer than one hundred votes.
18. Here Nettleford alludes to the poignant alternative Rastafari critiques that arose from a cadre of bright but disadvantaged individuals who did not get to further their schooling formally because of a lack of places but they alternatively found themselves arriving at deeper insights and comments about the society.
19. Jamaica's first and only premier, 1959–1962.
20. The impact of the Rastafari research done by Nettleford was demonstrated as early as 1964 through his Jamaica National Dance Theatre Company's production "Two Drums for Babylon". He admits this was somewhat prophetic as it anticipated the appeal of the Rastafari to the non-marginalized society and the middle classes before it had actually begun.
21. Leading Jamaican newspaper established in 1832.
22. He was vice chancellor of the University of the West Indies at the time that he gave this speech.
23. Nettleford at this point paused to take questions, the first one being on the matter of Rastafari and the timing of repatriation.
24. Here Nettleford plays on the Christian images of the concept of heaven as a land in the sky with honey and milk in abundance.
25. According to Nettleford, Garvey reportedly said these words in October 1937, in Menelik Hall in Nova Scotia, Canada. Later, Bob Marley took those words and transformed them into a powerful couplet, "None but ourselves can free our minds."
26. Walter Rodney, a Guyanese national, was a lecturer at the University of the West Indies who was banned from returning to Jamaica in October 1968 because the government of the day thought his involvement in Black Power activism was problematic for the state. Rodney was an avowed socialist who worked with the poor of Jamaica in an attempt to raise their political and cultural consciousness.

Chapter 2

Polite Violence

Mortimo Planno

Igziabeher y'massegan Haile Selassie.[1] In our beginning we start with our God, and in our ending with the Lord's name. So I greet you all and thank you for being present here, this time to listen to this talk on "polite violence".[2] Now it is a pleasure for me to describe "polite violence" in the manner I choose to describe it. In a *folk filosofi*.[3]

What the Brethren Wanted

Now 1954 – there was an artist in America, her name was Maymie Richardson,[4] who went to Ethiopia to do a command performance for His Majesty Haile Selassie I. And when she had done that command performance she left and came to Jamaica and gave out a message that [His Imperial Majesty] Haile Selassie I send to the Rastafarian – describing us as those boys with the beard – "Tell them I love them so much." We happen to be under violence – brutality from our society. [This is undeniable, and] those present old enough know what is present[ed] is [the] brutal truth – we the Rastafarian brethren in Jamaica could not walk or move about freely in our society, [the society which] some of us born into. We were intimidating by our presence. People intimidated just because them see a Rastaman. We made a verbal appeal to the students and teachers of this [University of the West Indies (UWI), which was] only twelve years old at the time . . . now fifty years old –

soon golden jubilee. What the students and teachers did was to make a survey of the Rastafarian movement in Kingston to find out what the Rastafarian brethren want and what the UWI can do for us. What we know it could do for us is to explain in their terms what the Rastafari brethren want – we wanted the world at large, starting [with] Jamaica, to tell the world that the Rastafari brethren want to go back to Africa, which we call "repatriation".

Repatriation

The Jamaican society did not want that of the Rastafarian brethren. They did not even want we to want that. But we were able to use our wit and our wisdom to get the principality, which is the university, higher education, to tell the powers, which is the politician, that [what] all these brethren want is applicable too [i.e., what is their right], since 1948, [with the] Universal Declaration of Human Rights . So . . . the UWI students and professors, who know what . . . the Rastafarian wanted was tenable, . . . suggested . . . the government [do] a survey [conducted] by Professor Nettleford, just Rex Nettleford at the time, Sir Roy Augier and Mike Smith. Them time Mike Smith was doing a fellowship in Zaria, northern Nigeria. And he came over to Jamaica, [to the] UWI. He was a researcher that Professor Lewis[5] selected to do the survey. This survey . . . was just [done in] Kingston and [a] small [section along the] border [of] Spanish Town, it was not the entire island or [every] Rastafarian they surveyed. They did not have . . . much Rastafarian present. But it was like a seed that was planted and counted for generations.[6]

For what we ha[d] done is we ha[d] exposed this polite violence, through our wit and wisdom, to the world. The student that Dr Lewis asked to do the survey did so in quick time – three weeks – and presented to us, the Rastafarian, a draft of what you, the brethren, say you want and what [the government] can afford, with recommendation, that you get now. All Rastafari brethren wanted was repatriation!

Garvey Tell You Much about Back to Africa

By repatriation we mean to leave Jamaica and go back to Africa; . . . "back to Africa" was not any strange saying to the people of Jamaica. Sometimes me call you hypocrite, for you praise Marcus Garvey, for you hear Marcus Gar-

HIM Emperor Haile Selassie I

vey tell you much about back to Africa, [so this concept] was not strange to you people in Jamaica. But how it was applied, what it meant to some of you . . . what we notice? We notice it touchable! That middle-class, upper-middle-, middle-middle-middle [class] children began to [be] attracted to our fascination [with Africa and worldview]. First – fascinating walk.[7] The tourist board advertise in America, "Come to Jamaica and watch the Rastafarian walk." That mean we became a fascination, our walk, our mannerism, we walk with [our] head up high – that again fascinated you. The man who Garvey tell us can't look you in the eye. When the white man start talk to the black man in Jamaica them time – him [the black man] used to use him toe and dig the ground and look pon the ground all the while. Him did not have that . . . power to look into the white man eye. We developed that – that . . . backbone we didn't have swift start grow that . . . we have it today in society, [we even have a] black man who is . . . prime minister. What an achievement. And all that happen through Rasta, as simply as you tek it. "We going walk with Rasta."

Watch some of these polite violence. You know our educational system tell you about magic words such as "please", "sorry", "thank you", "excuse me". It gives them an opportunity to mash out your big toe and tell you, "Oh sorry sir!" We see it happen with one of our own brethren Bob Marley. Bob Marley suffered football injury in him big toe. Some writer who study, say was deliberate that them mash Bob Marley toe in a football match – we call it polite violence. Mash out Bob big toe and tell him "excuse" – and mek him carry a sore toe for three years, wrap up daily until our doctor discover it becoming cancerous, a special form of cancer. In this polite violence we going show you how doctor made mistake. I will use myself as an example of the guinea pig.

[In] 1961 when we came back from [our trip to] Africa – 4 April 1961 to 3 June 1961 – [we] went [almost immediately] to America on a series of lectures [to speak] about the trip we went on . . . [the] opportunity of going to Africa, which states in Africa would take us and things. After returning from America to Jamaica, I developed a virus in my throat – weh dem call thyroid glands problem – and I went to de hospital and mi locks and beard were in the position that it is now. And the doctor, surgeon – won't call him name now – one of the junior doctor is here with us who usually give the checks . . . No, not you [Dr Chevannes[8]], you were a reverend – but we have a medical doctor today now who was a junior doctor dem time. He noticed that the examination deh do to find out if me have thyroid glands problem was just a use you eye and do the test. I had a very serious goitre, a iceberg – you know the type of iceberg goitre what sink the Titanic? One of those type of goitre – not show[ing] outside as some people who grow the goitre and have the goitre hanging out, but one which was [hidden inside and] blocking up the throat. It wasn't really a goitre that growing nothing, blocking up . . . nothing more than one of the glands swell ten times the size of the other gland. Now, [they made] a dangerous mistake in just looking at me and saying, well, you need certain prescription and dem just look at me and start prescribe. So dem notice me start deteriorate, lose weight rapidly – now I gain weight terribly, want shed some, you understand. I was the sickest patient on my ward and didn't know . . . dem put me nearer to the nurse, and put a scale there and I have to weigh every day. [After I came out, they] tek me [back] in hospital fourteen different occasions before dem finally did this operation. That 1966 when Haile Selassie came to Jamaica was about the same time [I had the operation] – the throat did not even well up yet and oozing blood still. So a lot of mystic things start happening now. I suppose to get a prescription [because] the body short of iodine, so I must get twenty-nine drops of iodine as the prescription. Well we try keep up to that as a patient until dem decide fi do this operation. Now the first thing this doctor-surgeon want to do is to cut off mi locks. Wonder if you know how much a Rastaman love him locks? Anyhow, I will tell you bout dat later on. It was more than a polite violence to cut my locks – so I tell him nay, no I not going cut my locks. Him say, but you going dead. I say, I don't care – "What a damn fool, doh eeh?" So you know we have we connections? I write a Prof who is my Queen College University doctor friend – and complain to him – saying I can't understand yuh doctor business. Doctor say mi must cut off mi locks fi cut goitre. Him sey hair dangerous [in] dem type of operation business. They took seven and three-quarter hours to pare nine-tenth of the business [the goitre] – which is, all these things is, doctor error. Layman don't know these things is error of doctor and they should be more than compensated. In compensating mi, [they] mek mi a "fellow" of this university and things like that . . .

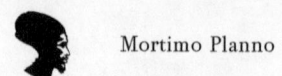
Mortimo Planno

A New Faculty of Education: Rastafari Raising Consciousness

We brought to the attention of you people – Jamaican society we a talk now – how dem [police] use arbitrary arrest as one of the [types of] violence, brutality as another [type of] violence and then dem total eclipse – [they] start deliberately kill us now. You find [one] Rasta dead deh so, you find [another] Rasta dead deh so, you find [a third] Rasta deh so dead. Nobody going go tend to him, nobody going care bout him, nobody going investigate wah cause him death and things. Anyhow, if I should go on in detail fi tell you how dis polite violence go, you can't believe people wicked so to dem one another. It was Dr Lewis who . . . explain it to Professor Nettleford dem – saying deal with this Rasta business, as a result of which the university never ever get recognition like when it deal in it. Polite violence. It going need a new faculty of education fi really see what polite violence is and how smart this Rastaman is.

The Report Recommendation: "Unworthy of Scholars"

The recommendation of the fact-finding survey that the student mek, cause the government to recommend . . . that . . . a fact-finding mission [should be sent] to Africa. Monsignor Wilson, Roman Catholic, first – I am not discriminating against the religion – but I want you find out . . . what . . . people did [when they learned of the recommendations of the report]. Monsignor Wilson said [about] the report . . . , "You mean you going ask us to give Rasta gold spoon?"[9] But nuh a man rights? But Monsignor, what these people say dem want you must tek it and give dem on a platter? You have radical students start show a touch of recognizing people freedom. So they say – give the Rastaman wah him want. Monsignor Wilson say, it unworthy fi scholars. Dem can't tek the report all right.

That time, [there was an] archbishop, canon – weh him name? – "Vernon", [who had spent] forty-one years in Nigeria, a place name Calabar, teaching ([and] now we have Calabar[10] as college, high school) . . . So one of the recommendations was to send a fact-finding mission to Africa – but we must

[not] mek a politician lead it – and they were thinking in terms of making this old canon – [who had] live[d] in Africa for forty-one years – lead it, Vernon.

We are about to go Africa now (too much time can go, if we go in detail as to what and what happen), but dem mek a PNP [politician], Dr Leslie[11] go – him run as mayor and was PNP [member of parliament] in Spanish Town and Linstead in St Catherine . . . Him go university dat when him speak in Africa – and see how him haffi do him neck – you would not like fi see it – now a deh the problem deh.[12] The first thing we observe is that no care how you train in this university, when you reach Africa you going haffi go right back a dis African university which is the sidewalk university in Africa; you haffi go right back to you tribe fi learn how fi nyam instead a eat. For you stop learn fi nyam. Weh you use culture[13] – now [as a tool for adjustment and survival]. For you have two hand, yeah, but you only use one fi put a you mouth, for the next one use as toilet paper, or [if] no paper . . . use water and wash yourself [with that other hand] after you go toilet more dem use tissue paper wipe yourself which you no properly wipe up when you use toilet paper compare with when you use water [using water to wash after using the toilet is more hygienic than use of toilet paper]. It is a culture – and we did not start realize that now until we learn it, and see deh, you call these thing . . . culture shock. Dem there was so much culture shocking coming out of the report of the . . . fact-finding mission which we send go Africa.

The recommendation of the UWI was to send a mission to Africa, but you must send prominent Rastafarian, that was Morti Planno – and [the mission] point out dat the *Phyllis Wheatley*,[14] one of Marcus Garvey's ship dock up in a de ocean in Monrovia in Liberia right now, those who know our ship weh use to down a Greenwich Farm name *Old Lorna* weh couldn't pay tax and leave deh go deh through seizure – some of the same [experience] as *Phyllis Wheatley*, one of Marcus Garvey back to Africa ship. For what happened is we did not wait to get money or ask fi sponsorship – rich man who sponsor African fi send dem go a Africa. As we get the opportunity we use it, use it fi carry one foot forward – everytime an opportunity open we go through that door and call down African pon dem. Mek I show you what I am trying to say for you might don't understand.

Marcus Garvey learn from Mohammed Ali that the people in the Caribbean want to learn more about Africa. And him, Marcus Garvey, did not have the language to tell it to the people. Him didn't really have that approach. The Rastaman, for instance, have a better approach than him in that day at telling the

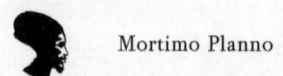

Mortimo Planno

people about back to Africa, than tell[ing] the people about [the] Middle Passage and how slavery goes and hav[ing] to explain to you who can't read.

Now I going use some dates. Ms Richardson came here in 1954 [and she] perform for Haile Selassie, [singing] "Play on your harp little David, play on your harp". Now Haile Selassie is little David and she a sing play on your harp. Now see Brother Brown mek a harp[15] out deh you go look what Brother Brown have outside and you will see what we really dealing with. This art and craft.[16]

The Mission: Polite Violence in Government

Rastaman is some of the greatest art and craft students and professors in the world [although] him don't realize that. But anyhow, we went to Nigeria – where Dr Smith mek certain that this fact-finding mission go up north where he was studying at the time – [to] a place name Zaria. Now, first thing we notice – [bear in mind] we have on pretty pants, for is all tropical trousers dem mek we go down London shop and buy at about twenty per cent less – when we go [is] the people dem in Zaria don't wear clothes, dem don't have on no robe, no nothing like that. Immediately you can hear members of our delegation say, Den mek mi ask oonu something? A dem place oono want fi come live? [Laughter.]

Polite violence, you know. But dem don't understand yet we sey yes. But we go a next place – apart from Zaria – we go Enugu, weh we buck upon all "Ahmadu Bello" Sardauna of Sokoto,[17] and dem was trained politicians who learn to have political parties and thing like dat and have some particular attitudes more than you politicians who claim you are politicians out yah. For the tribal business in Africa is politically different from the tribalism we have in Jamaica politically. Anyhow, but is learn we a learn, for is fact-finding. The Jamaica government send Vic Reid as one who would do a comprehensive report – secretary of the fact-finding while we go along. Him was a deputy leader of this delegation weh we went to Africa wid. We notice we went [to] five African-speaking state of Africa who have British High Commission, true [i.e., because] it is English-speaking African state dem [that] have British embassies and high commission. We notice [that at the end of] every . . . day the ambassador or high commissioner, white man now you know – please white people I am not saying these things [out of] prejudice, these are fact-finding – invite a part of our delegation, like Dr Leslie, Vic Reid, to tea party.

A White Man at Every Table

For every prime minister's table there is a white man who is secretary general or permanent secretary for something. But all him a do is fi use him eye and use him report fi tell dem how we operate. Good. When we come back from Africa, Norman Manley, our prime minister then, say I must give him [a] report since him been getting report sey on the whole way I was not satisfied [with] what was going on. I must give dem a report about what went on [in] the delegation. So I said whole heap of bad word. "I naw give you no report. If you did want we give you report, follow what Dr Lewis say!" Dr Lewis sey, don't mek a politician carry these people. Because dem going sey we doing it fi get vote. That time I had no intention to vote fi dem either. And we wasn't any opposition to dem either, we were just extremists. Somebody going have to say no! And no care how you don't feel good about it, . . . somebody going have to say no. And me take the opportunity. See the pay off?

We learn for – see my teacher in audience Ziguy[18] – him came thirty years ago to Jamaica. From Ethiopia, to this same UWI, night after night we were having classes at the UWI. Trying to teach we one and two Amharic word. But at the same time him want to know where we get this zeal from for Africa, for Garvey sey so. Garvey have two million delegate/candidate member of the UNIA back to Africa movement. [But on the mission to Africa] the Rastaman was only represented by three, so somebody going have to be resolute to take all of the violence, politely, and try respond to it in this time.

We want to bring to your consideration the term . . . violence. You going do the Jamaican society [violence?] That is why the people crying out now – you going treat dem like how you treat the Rasta? When dem did believe you weren't going to treat dem [violent] way, [the ordinary people now] have to tek Rasta side – what a pity! You didn't realize sey people would resist as how they resisting now? . . . Ganja, for instance, the British colonial master only give you six months in prison, for no care what amount of ganja dem find you with in dat society. In this society when dem sey we get independence and freedom and all dem thing deh, you know weh the penalty for ganja right now? All death. Yes!

Then that is more than polite violence.

Michael Manley go in prison and leggo people who smoke a spliff. For him explain it sey when we driving up Russell Heights, Graham [Heights], Arcadia[19] and [in] dem heights [you] smell the ganja [because people there are] smoking on the verandahs . . . verandahs [that] have on some nice

Mortimo Planno

chairs – you know, when like [the] Chinese man . . . used to use him board and cotch up him head when him smoke him opium – . . . [but the police turn a blind eye]. Now, how you St Andrew people smoke the ganja pon the verandah and no police no stop? For first thing, if the police stop, him lose him job. [If the police should choose to accost ganja smokers in those residential communities] by time [the police] fi drive off, dem tek him number and report him, sey him interfere with tourist who dem sey dem must be unmolested. So the politicians dem buy out these apartments dem up deh – Russell [Heights], Graham Heights . . . Perkins Heights and Zadie Place,[20] and dem kind of twenty-six families have some "con-dem-monium" houses big like hotel a rent out to these people who become problem to dem today. [Yet, they] burn down our tattoo[21] weh we live and call it slum area or inner city or old car. It is the truth my brethren.. Your father was a judge . . . your two brother[s] [were] lawyer[s] – is so the whole of dem support that discriminat[ion] gainst you and sey we mad dem pickney with ganja. Don't it?[22]

Coral Garden[23] – all different kind of garden now. For the polite violence is how dem treat we and how we react.

We sey respect. If they had respected the opinion of these little people they would [not] be in this mess today. For dem can't get way either. I going show you why dem can't get weh. [I] have to associate mi self with it too. We have an ACP[24] business, going work out – find market fi people we a ask fi produce more. The product we going produce is food. And the market is to sell to those who don't have no food . . . Yet still we [have companies] like GraceKennedy[25] . . . [who import food like] pumpkin. Can you imagine [they] import pumpkin [and] cabbage? GraceKennedy import all that mek fi him product. And we have land here [to grow the food ourselves], but you don't give the people dem none. But later on you expect we to support a ACP product – making a market fi these product when we do farm? We a go farm fi sell [to] those who have no food? And hear what you do now, you mek president of Zimbabwe chairman of dem programme. America carry 102 including dem president of Africa. Who we are suppose to be doing the programme for? . . . it is people who don't have any food we supposed to a plant and mek food fi dem.

So we Rasta would glad fi support programme like those – stay hungry, for I would a loose the weight and able fi walk – without me being carried around like a baby. But it is a disease wey – I notice, I get a glimpse on the TV, where you have all the Pope a suffer with the same type of walking problem – people have to a carry him like me. You think is joke [laugh]. You watch the TV when you go home back. You find one week you have some big name – is not boast we a boast sey dem dead lef we you know – man like Sherlock, Issa, who dead Jerry – one week – Matalon, Mary, Dianne, Queen Daughter and the Catholic Mother Theresa. And the whole bungle of dem set of people and all dem things start happen – good.[26]

Weh we would like Dr Chevannes and me glad or can't tell you thanks no more or louder – and dem did hold you in dis predicament – so me and you hand cuff like how American do fi dem kind of prisoner. Two of we a prisoner, police and thief. A so American police carry go a jail you know? Handcuff de pon him, so is that dem we put we in a di car and we gone a jail. Me no really want call dem name for dem easy fi vex more than we. Sorry Sir! But darling I love you, you know that you lie but excuse me! You understand? And use these words "love" and "marriage" and "days of our lives" and "bold and beautiful", dem type of opera to show we fi dem life.[27]

Well, we want to see if these performances have use to the situation. And we pick out Bob Marley as one of our performer who do command performance for every country in the world. And we tek it and say carry it forward. We use Dr Chevannes, we use Rex Nettleford, we use Mike Smith, we use Roy Augier, for dem [the government] give him all [the knighthood and the resulting title] "Sir" you know. Good.

Dem a go give you "Sir", Prof [Chevannes]?

[Dr Chevannes responds]: No!

You a rebel then.

Well, dem have some of who dem give "Sir" – dem give me fellow. Can you imagine a thing like that? Rebel with cause and rebel without cause! You understand. And we see how much of the thing weh dem expect we fi carry this millennium to 2000, in this twenty-first century, with this type of society – you watch dem outside there – is not "art" dem a look fi buy or "thoughts" dem a look fi sell. And then you see dem gone down to where prime minister [P.J. Patterson] deh. Prime minister might all come down here before me done talk – him good fi talk to – and you see how dem full up in here and dem no mean it. Can you imagine the exhibition we see outside there and the audience we see inside here? We satisfied? We can't satisfied. Me can't tell you move closer together that the camera can tek you sey you did listen what is polite violence.

But we understand how we share. For this is one of our problems, you know sir – we can't share. The first black one weh dem mek chair, a "Shearer"[28] him name you know? Him can't share in the world of no blood bath. Him

Mortimo Planno

can't share for we learnt some story. When Rasta 1958, [19]59, [19]60, get this terrible polite violence approach, it is from the PNP you know.[29] When we go to prime minister and prime minister lean back so and sey: "How we a go Africa?"

We sey in Victorian Days, Victoria leave twenty million pounds . . . for we to go. Him sey no. "No! No! It was good St George the IV", and him go bring one book like the table top tall so with chain and padlock pon it and open it in front of him so and start read before him even find the page, say, "Good King William grant twenty million pounds for indentured slave."

Him sey, "You know you slaves were property of the white man?"

We say, "Come on man." Mi sey, "Where the slave master deh now?"

Him sey, "They all died out!"

Mi sey, "Naw sa and mi a one of the slave."

Him sey, "Come Morti – you do understand this you know – we can't just let you go so, no care how you broke. For you value more as a slave here than money. We can send you pon any mission go influence Rasta, call dem up a you university mek dem fellow, dem will glad fi dat."

No sah, we glad yes, but you know Barry [Chevannes], we still want to go Africa.

Bad Mind

A one mind we have in the Caribbean and outside of Africa – is "bad mind". But in Africa you have gold mine – weh . . . Marco Polo, Ameri, Christopher [Columbus] dem leave from all bout come look fi those mines, gold mines. Dem find all different kinds of mines when dem come [there] – green gold (gold have all different kinds of colours), [i.e. banana green gold], cane as another gold, bauxite as next gold . . .

And we must not . . . revolt against these things. For it may be too much a harsh word fi use bout revolution.

For Jerry [Small] is the first I ever see people who resolute so – these youth of today. You kill dem today, you can't kill dem tomorrow so dem prefer dead today. I rather dead with the young one rather [than the] old. Mi a old man, mi sick and blood stop circulate – and me want live. All Bob Marley sey it. Him feel like him would bomb up the church when him find the parson is lying and the pastor admit sey, "We do lie sometimes."

We really want give you some opportunity fi ask. For me want ask Barry fi ask me certain questions too. If me satisfied that within a couple days' time we going into the twenty-first century? For we talk about 1998, 1996, but 1999 the next year going 2000. But we don't know we approaching a very serious time. [Take] 1977 [for example] – when the three sevens clash.[30] Is the same year dem sey Bustamante dead. Nineteen ninety-nine now I don't know who going dead. Dem going sey is we kill dem.

All baby, who baby do anything sir? Baby responsible for any of these problems? Yet still, dem programme from December 1973 was repeal of the abortion law. Free ooman fi throw way baby? That caan possible? The doctor say the abortionist, and dem type of druggist deh mek more money than you man with PhD and faculty studies behind your name.

Dem go bank manager, im friend. Want some money fi borrow, fi do certain kind of business. Him sey, come Dr Chevannes, you don't have to borrow no money, man. Myrie out a Spanish Town road who dash weh belly, dem mek more money than you. I don't know if I going find the correct words Dr Chevannes fi tell you a story, now, how Kitty Breeze, a call girl, dem middle class call girl, dem keep she fi sustain and accommodate the West Indies cricket team. For you only have two [institutions with] West Indi[es in the name] at dem time – UWI and West Indies cricket team. So when West Indies play in cricket dem have some call girl who is the wife of so and so – we give dem the touch weh dem want. Dem happen fi find the captain of the West Indies cricket team a wife, for get everything included in your package, when you become a tourist and come on tour you get a package, including a woman, beautiful Jamaican woman . . . Little Jamaica, win Miss World, more than once. So Jamaica have pretty woman in the world and all over the world.

That if you look in the newspaper this week there you see dem a trade a Miss World. Polite violence. The woman leg dem, dem tek it and mek it a new brand leg. And judge her by that. Walk! And she walk down the aisle . . . best leg. You, Barry, vote twenty-four fi the best leg. "What a pretty leg you have eeh?"

Big fat ooman now, who have fourteen pickney, you no bodder count she, for she can't come count pon your beauty contest. Yet she sustain the race, something bigger than trained leg, girl who just keep her head so and shut up her two eye . . . And two time [Jamaicans won Miss World]. The first time dem going have a revolutionary Miss World is when the government of Jamaica sey don't attend no Miss World contest! And Cindy[31] sey, "No boy, mi aago go." And she go and win. Weh you think dem do? Marry she to the dreadlocks Rastaman.[32] Can you imagine a thing like that? So you have here . . . Mr World, a dreadlocks man, Rastaman, and Miss World, a rebel who defy her government. Her government sey no and she sey yes. But here is the politician now? Him no want nobody but Miss World – for [example] A.G.S. Coombs's[33] wife use to go a beef market with him and carry a quarter cow. By the time you mek him minister, you know which part she deh, Barry? Asylum. For him no want she no more. Yes. You go inna di asylum, you don't see whole heap a old woman a talk to themselves?

"Bblaw, bblaw ahh."

When you ask dem "Weh you grandson/son?"

"Barry Chevannes doctor at university."[34]

"You understand?"

You despise you grandmother, your grandaunt, because she too old. She feeble like me. And [when they] walk, people have to a carry dem . . . University [Hospital] and KPH[35] are two different hospital now, but one of dem doctors here, Barry, tell me say one time [they] have antibiotics weh can get you better within twenty-four hours? But dem have to thinking whether to use antibiotics on you little dutty Rasta man fi get you better within twenty-four hours. [But they gave it to] Dr Lecky and Professor Sherlock and Dr Sherlock who mek anthem, fi . . . keep dem alive for three months and it don't mean nothing for us. All dem look and see [is] Rastaman. Trouble-maker. I happen to spend two months in Lagos, Nigeria, [having been] invited there by my professor brethren. You are my brethren too you know Barry. But you is only professor at the UWI, college of the West Indies, what only have six thousand or so students. But my professor in Africa there now, him a professor of [a] university, who have millions of students. And you have some who follow some of these fellow and underrate us Rasta. But you have some who follow to the T, appreciate what you do, write me letter and sey . . . to thank the professors who tek a second look at the value of Rasta brethren. We also in Africa will have to take a second look at the value of you Rastafarian in Jamaica, so we welcome you back home.

Now, as polite violence grow hotter . . . it no polite any more. Dem start open prison door, and let we inna prison. Dem start recognize the prisoner sey dem can tek horn and give a man in prison and sey talk to the people who live outside of the prison.[36] Can you imagine a thing like that? Something synonymous [with what] dem did me. Him Imperial Majesty come to Jamaica and the zeal of the people overwhelm and crowd up the plane. And

Polite Violence

you did not fire. But the protocol was broken down. And to restore it you had to find someone to do that. Fortunately for the dreadlocks Rastaman, dem come and call him police, brigadier.

"Calling Mr Planno."

"Calling Mr Planno."

Emperor call you. Mi sey, what? Barry you would like see – is pon a house top I deh you know, [like] "Zacchaeus".[37] Is pon a house top out at the airport I deh and hear brigadier come off the plane right to which part me deh and sey the emperor call me. Can you imagine? Me tek one step and it's pon the plane mi reach. After me greet His Majesty, the governor general ask me, "Mortimo, can you get your brethren to move from around the plane, mek His Majesty alight." Mi sey, yes if you give me the [same horn[38]] ya. Shearer, Sangster[39] sey no, if you go give him the horn him a go chant [laugh], so can you imagine if dem give me the horn and me start sey "Rastaman Vibration yeah ahh!!!" it [would] mek the chaos more! You understand? So dem had to put up with it fi just wait till the right time come and me ask you, "Mi brethren, His Majesty want to come down" so dem just open the way and his majesty come off. No problem.

Dem start market on dem t-shirts, "Jamaica. No problem."

All we right now a teach *folk filosofi*. It turn right back.

But here is a doctor (him in Canada [now]) whey, when him a junior doctor . . . down KPH, [he was] very sympathetic to the Rastaman. You can sey him is the only sympathetic Rastaman out deh, [though] him no have no locks. And Dr Street – him do fifteen years in Ethiopia, as doctor – him deh a Portland; him love all what Brother Brown[40] go on with, him support Brother Brown artwork. All Scott[41] dem people love art whether dem love the colour or the prowess of Brother Brown [or not].

But weh we glad fi see is at least me self and Brother Brown is two reminder. For you have a lot of brethren who was around who drop out and glad fi see all Brother Brown how strong him is, stronger than me. Look pon Brother Brown and [how] him walk [up] Murray Mountain.[42] Look pon all dem thing him exhibit out there. Is him do it, you know!? Dem tek Brother Brown from here – send go exhibition – show off pon him and no give him nothing. Mi nuh know how Jah put it in to your heart that you can mek dem even come look pon some of his exhibits. Brother Brown use fi live behind examination depot. All when the emperor come, nothing. Dem have him in a little corner. Thank you fi bringing him out. And thank him fi bring me out too.

Mortimo Planno

And we all thank the UWI students and professors for where dem reach in following us Rasta. We show dem that some people don't know who is a brain from who is a brawn. Brother Brown, you younger than me right now, yet still you seven years older than me. But my teacher come whisper in my ears – sey him get mix up in your family – Haile Selassie who did send him as our teacher – him mix up in your family him have children.[43]

You see when him bring the water?[44] When mi a come down. Polite violence. That mi a show you.

Me just listen Haile Selassie speech weh sey him admire Canada, for him have seven teachers from Canada, working in Ethiopia. Him don't have seven from Jamaica. We should have more than seven teachers from Jamaica and the Caribbean who do research, working in Ethiopia right now for Haile Selassie, 1974, 1972, I go pay a visit to Ethiopia. As [soon] as I go to the hotel, out of his presence, about half dozen generals . . . come fi ask me if is plan we out yah a plan invasion of Ethiopia. I was surprise.

I was at Ward Theatre[45] when Michael Manley come, come watch one of Nettleford's dance. And when him watch it him come backstage. Him sey, Mortimo don't mek dem influence you. Mi sey, What dat mean sir? Him sey, somehow or the other is like him see a bauxite[46] – mi no know bout politics – him give me an education within five minutes. [He told me] dat Bustamante sell the bauxite [for] one shilling a ton. I go Africa go see iron ore fifty-five shillings a ton. Smelt it down and mek one of dem car tongue wah lock the bonnet. We pay six pounds for that and buy a ton of iron ore for one shilling.[47] The bauxite sold in Jamaica by Bustamante [was] one shilling a ton and PNP people and him a row out a street, and [the people] sey, You sell the Jamaican bauxite for one shilling? You give weh the people dem inheritance. Him [Busta] sey, "If I did not sell it somebody else would sell it. If dem had stayed inside somebody else would come out."

Manley father, Norman, him was able to get nine shilling a ton for bauxite and Michael get forty-one shilling a ton fi bauxite – and get money out of bauxite. Now, ganja – the police [have] full control of ganja. Him price it, him look market, him do everything for ganja – him plant it, him lock you up. And that is ganja, which dem sey is the best profit you can mek – but who you think is in charge of that? Police! Can you imagine you tek puss, call dem cat if you want to watch cheese?[48] The police mek the price of ganja. Him do the farming. If you think is joke me a mek, go home and watch news tonight and you see how much acre of ganja, a fire – but during the said fire weh dem a bun the ganja [by way of police raids on fields] with

Polite Violence

you find some of the best farmer, police farmer, tek him bayonet and mek some farrow and roll up some kali bud gone strike dem – polite violence – political violence, in a little society like his we want to see Dr Chevannes, if within couple more days to end 1998 – we have a whole year in 1999 to watch the changes of dem polite violence. If you going mek the twenty-six family work out to (the) you nuh know nothing bout cricket – so me can't call you in it. But you see the Prescot family, man who a correctional man him name John Prescot. Joe Prescot, George Prescot, Mr Prescot mi tell you fi watch it.

Forbes – commission – police – TV analysis Forbes, nurse Forbes – family affairs start come down on mi – we use to call dem Ashenheim, Jones, Webster, Mill [will] holder,[49] dem crap up everything and mek Mutty Perkins have whole villa for himself. Perkins Garden, Zadie Garden – nothing for the poor. I don't hear nothing of a Chevannes Garden yet. Dem naw give me no garden, for my garden done reap already.

Polite violence is my topic. Me going leave you here fi see if you understand.

Mi doctor leave Canada fi come see me – sey him want touch mi.

Is not me name Lazarus who throw bomb down Gordon House. But dem had a mysterious bombing [so] dem start call me and other name – shoot out mouth pon one another and Lazarus come from the grave and dash bomb a Gordon House. You know weh going happen? You going deh a Canada and hear sey hell broke out. Polite violence – it no dat polite. Hear . . . him, "Dem now go do dat."

Me and Barry have one hell of [a] quarrel – I facety with him. When His Majesty [Barry] come down a Trench Town and ask me if me see my picture replica inna the Bible, me sey to him sey, "A de pope send him/Barry fi ask me dat?" So is like him sey no sah, no sah. Is like me a underrate him, sey him couldn't find that question himself but me did feel like a Bishop Maclanies send him come ask me. Mi know him forgive me – him sey him a read through him Bible and notice sey scripture guide him to someone [who] a go meet him up there.[50] I don't know if is on the tarmac or ramp, but I found myself taken up. Go meet His Majesty up there, and we call him God.

Our heaven was in a little plane there . . . Twenty-six writers write book bout me. One say Haile Selassie was so frighten to see these long[-haired] man come invade his plane that him run inside and lock the door and me single-handedly go open the door and, like a bad man, sey "Come", and carry him go King's House.

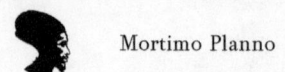

Mortimo Planno

So throughout this whole political violence – we have to do it in book form. But I want help to do. All comments send it come, whether me talk foolishness, wit or wisdom, we want you to send it come.[51] For people who like to read. What the Rastaman sey is polite violence.

Who is the idiot – Morti Planno? Or is it those who underrate Rasta? Dem burn a van, shub it inna the sea – not polite. Rastaman a drive the van, him get out a control, dem sey, and drive it inna a dancehall. Dem tek weh the key, tek him out, dead him – and shub weh the van and burn it, all that inna polite violence. Caribbean students sey it's no joke. While some people dancing the ska, Africa is burning, and you tek it as I tell you. I wish that within the one year and few day what will bring the twentieth century, where everything going end with naught [as in the year 2000] . . . you will learn what is polite violence.

Acknowledgements

This talk was given by Mortimo Planno at the Faculty of Social Science Lecture Theatre, University of the West Indies, Mona, November 1998.

Notes

1. Transliterated Amharic greeting, "Thanks be to God in the name of the Holy Trinity."
2. "Polite violence" is an oxymoronic concept developed by Mortimo Planno expounded here anecdotally to convey his and other Rastafari experience with Western civil society. It articulates how the official society continuously uses subtle and civil measures to discriminate and victimize Rastafari – in a way to cause violence unto these individuals.
3. This piece has been transcribed from an oral address. Planno, in this address, speaks in a combination of standard English and patois (or patwa). The transcription has been edited for clarity. Planno's discursive style is what ethnographer Carole Yawney describes as being driven by synchronicity, so throughout his conversation he pulls on incidents and activities which converge within specific time and space.
4. This is an African American singer who was also the international organizer

of the Ethiopian World Federation. She came to Jamaica in the mid-1950s to sensitize persons about the ideas expounded through the Ethiopian World Federation.
5. Sir Arthur Lewis.
6. Planno here argues that the survey was limited in its scope and did not take into account a large cross section of Rastafari – the movement he argues was an indelible part of the spirit of the African Jamaican that has survived for ages.
7. Here Planno alludes to the Rastafari aesthetics generally and the defiant gait and stride of the rude-boy/rebel.
8. The lecture "Polite Violence" took place in the Faculty of Social Sciences, University of the West Indies and was chaired by Barry Chevannes, then dean of the faculty. Planno makes constant reference to him throughout the conversation – at times seemingly almost like a dialogue directed at the dean.
9. Planno poses the question concerning the idea of investigating the interest in repatriation. He then uses "Monsignor" as his interlocutor as an illustration of the opposition to Rastafari rights.
10. Calabar refers to a fifteenth-century port town in southeastern Nigeria that the members of the 1961 mission to Africa visited. The Jamaican high school of the same name was established just over one hundred years ago and is named after that town.
11. This is a reference to Dr L.C. Leslie, a medical doctor and People's National Party activist, who led the first mission to Africa. Other members of the delegation were Messrs Filmore Alvaranga, Douglas Mack, Mortimo Planno, Westmore Blackwood, Cecil Gordon, Monroe Scarlett, Victor Reid and Dr M.B.J. Douglas.
12. Planno here registers one of his consistent criticisms of the character of the mission he went on in 1961 – particularly as it concerned the attitudes of the Jamaican officials towards Africa and the Africans – suggesting that they the Jamaican officials were so Western elitist in their orientation that the potential connections that the trip should have engendered were undermined.
13. Planno here uses "culture" as a term to mean a repository of innate knowledge.
14. This refers to the SS *Phyllis Wheatley*, Marcus Garvey's second Black Star Line ship, named after the eighteenth-century African American poet.
15. Reference to a multi-dimensional work called Dove Harp by Brother Everald Brown, spiritual artist, in an exhibition entitled "A Passage with the

Elders" which complemented Planno's lecture, Exhibition, UWI, Mona, November 1998.

16. This is yet another example of the synchronic style of Planno – where he is establishing a type of "magical realism", wherein the connection between the emperor and the Rastafari is anchored on a deeper communication that allows for the manifestation of the Rastafari vision and desires.

17. Ahmadu Bello Sardauna of Sokoto, first premier of the Northern Nigeria region (1954–1966).

18. Referring to his Amharic language teacher, Ziguy.

19. These are areas in St Andrew, Jamaica, considered to be the abode of the wealthy.

20. Planno argues that the place names honour and represent the legacy of the rich. All these communities, in Planno's estimation, have connections to the names of privileged Jamaicans.

21. This is patois for makeshift shanty housing, usually from zinc and cardboard.

22. This is Planno identifying Robin "Jerry" Small in the audience, who emerged from a black middle-class family – and by Planno's account was an example of the class tensions displayed by the upper class, especially when members of their ranks became a part of the Rastafari movement.

23. Coral Gardens is a district in the parish of St James just outside of the city of Montego Bay where, in 1963, the government conducted a manhunt, rounding up members of the Rastafari movement who were allegedly involved in an incident which claimed the lives of eight persons, including civilians and police.

24. This refers to the group created in 1975 to represent the African, Caribbean and Pacific group of states.

25. GraceKennedy is a local Jamaican food processing and packaging company.

26. Planno is making a general point about how wealth does not save people. The names mentioned are those of the rich and powerful. This idea is expressed in Planno's personal mode of communication.

27. After an additional thank you to Chevannes, Planno discusses the binary relationship between police and thieves as a metaphor for the relationship between the powerful and the powerless, and goes on to say that this is a modality that is represented in popular culture. Performing the obsequious, powerless role or the powerful role are just that, performances.

28. Planno here makes reference to former prime minister of Jamaica, Hugh Shearer (1967–1972).

Polite Violence

29. Planno here makes reference to a period of agitation among the brethren and reaction by the official society between 1958 and 1960. At this time character, such as Prince Emmanuel and Mortimo Planno feature – both of whom had been part of the organization for the first Rastafari groundation in Back-o-Wall – in March 1958. In the midst of this in October 1959 there was the Claudius Henry–led repatriation call which led hundreds of Rastafari to mobilize themselves in the city in anticipation of ships arriving to take them to Africa. This was partly the reason for the invitation to the university to survey the brethren in 1960. Planno makes the point that the PNP was at the helm of the countries leadership at this time and concludes that the PNP initiated this "polite violence" approach.
30. This is a reference to the seventh day of the seventh month in the year 1977 (i.e., 7/7/77), considered auspicious.
31. This is a reference to Cindy Breakspeare, Jamaican Miss World 1976.
32. This is a reference to the common-law union between Cindy Breakspeare and Bob Marley, made public by the announcement of the birth of their son Damian "Jr Gong" Marley.
33. Alan St Clavar Coombs was a militant Garveyite and co-founder of Jamaica Workers and Transport Union. His groundwork was instrumental to the success that politicians, such as Alexander Bustamante, were to subsequently enjoy through his leadership of the labour union.
34. Here Planno uses "Barry Chevannes" as an example of a prominent and successful Jamaican to make the case about the ungratefulness of the society to its core creators/providers.
35. Kingston Public Hospital.
36. Here Planno makes reference to what has been called the 1998 "Zeeks Riots" in West Kingston, when members of the community marched on the streets demanding the release of notorious area leader Donald "Zeeks" Phipps. The shock noted by Planno is that the prison officials, in a bid to quell the crowd's anger, released Zeeks unto a balcony at the Central Police Station in Kingston for him to address and disperse the crowd.
37. This is the biblical figure Zacchaeus, described as a short man who climbed up a sycamore fig tree so that he might be able to see Jesus.
38. Planno returns to history to make a comparison between the situation with Zeeks being given a "bullhorn" to quell the masses as being somewhat similar to his being given the same "bullhorn" at the time of the visit of the emperor to disperse the crowd that had gathered around the plane.

39. Donald Sangster was the deputy prime minister of Jamaica at the time of the visit of His Imperial Majesty Emperor Haile Selassie I to Jamaica.
40. Brother Everald Brown was an intuitive artist and early Rastafari teacher-leader who had mounted an exhibition of paintings and carvings at the time of Planno's lecture.
41. This is a reference to A.D. Scott, the Jamaican art collector.
42. Murray Mountain in St Ann was where Brother Brown lived and worked. This is close to Nine Miles, the same region which Bob Marley originated from.
43. Planno here is indicating that Ziguy (the Ethiopian Amharic teacher) told him that he had married into Brother Everald Brown's family and had children by that union.
44. Planno is offered water and he uses this as yet another opportunity to demonstrate the character of the polite violence – in other words, the courtesy is late, thus a form of polite violence.
45. The Ward Theatre is a venue for plays and cultural productions. It was opened in 1912, and is found in downtown Kingston, Jamaica.
46. Planno here uses "bauxite" as a metaphor for exploitation or a "sell out".
47. This is thought to be a hyperbole.
48. Planno is suggesting here that the police too have a love for ganja – as would a cat for cheese.
49. Planno seeks to position the state of the nation – akin to a nepotistic sell-out as people grab at riches for themselves and family.
50. Here Planno referes to the the famous picture of himself on the plane steps on the occasion of the visit of the emperor in 1966 – when he had to quell the excitement of he crowd. On this occasion of the lecture Planno argues that Chevannes first came to him to inquire about this moment as a prophetic instance that connected Rastafari to the Bible.
51. Here Planno references his desire to update his autobiographic record. One of the objectives of the visiting fellowship awarded to Planno was to facilitate his writing and documenting his life story.

Reference

Planno, Mortimo. 1996. *The Earth Most Strangest Man: The Rastafarian*. New York: Institute of Man, 1996.

Chapter 3

You Must Be Willing to Reason Together

Roy Augier

The only reason I am standing before you tonight is because I am the only living member of the group that wrote the *Report on the Rastafari Movement in Kingston, Jamaica*. And since this is the case, I would like us to begin by remembering Professor Mike Smith, Professor Rex Nettleford and also our colleague Mortimo Planno. I would like you to stand for a minute while in silence we remember these three men, two of whom honoured the university while they were alive by their work in anthropology, the other who brought distinction to the brethren by his life. Let us be silent for a minute.

Thank you.

I shall not be able to address you in the manner of those who preceded me to this microphone. You can see that I am a "bald head man". I am also a "university man". I would like to remark that what I learnt in the two weeks that I and Mike Smith and Rex Nettleford associated with the brethren to accumulate the material for the report was the capacity for the brethren to reason *together*. This university is not "U-Blind".[1] It never was, and you cannot build a fence around people if you invite them to reason together.

My full experience of associating with the brethren is the variety of opinion that they share. So tonight, I will behave as if I am again in 1960 reasoning with brethren. So, I will no doubt say some things that might not please some of you, but I expect you to receive what I say in the spirit of reasoning with me.

Because the organizers of this conference made the anniversary of the report the centre of the study that you will be doing in the next few days, they

Roy Augier

asked me to speak about the report. So I shall begin speaking about what in effect are *five* reports, although I will not attempt to talk in any detail about them – and in fact I'm sorry that you do not have the reports with you tonight. Those of you who are going to be here tomorrow will have the opportunity to receive them from those who have organized the conference. So you will pardon me if I begin with that, but I also want to go on after I have given you an account of the reports to say a few things which might be the musings – or the babblings – of a bald-head man in relation to the opinions, the beliefs, the social effects of Rastafari in the Jamaican society.

So let us begin with the report, and I again remind you that what I have to say may be, in some respects, in conflict with some things that you have heard. The report came about as a result of a letter, which I greatly regret that I'm not able to read to you tonight because the archives of the university have been put away because of a fire that took place in the room of the building in which they were stored; but what I have is the letter which Sir Arthur Lewis wrote to Norman Manley, and I will begin by reading that to you:

> My dear premier,[2]
> At the request of some of the prominent members of the Rastafari brethren, three members of the UCWI[3] staff, Roy Augier, Rex Nettleford and M.G. Smith, spent every day of two weeks with the Rastafari brethren making a survey of the movement, its organization and its aspirations. They have produced a report which I enclose herewith. The team has made a number of recommendations which require urgent consideration. The movement is large and in a state of great unrest. Its problems require priority treatment. Though the movement has no single leader or group of leaders, it is willing to produce a small group of prominent representatives to discuss with the government the recommendations contained in this report. I very much hope that we may be able to arrange such a meeting at the earliest possible opportunity.
> Yours truly,
> William Arthur Lewis
> Principal

This letter, from the principal of the UCWI to the premier of Jamaica, accompanied the report. I must tell those of you who do not know, that I am a historian – that we are accustomed to seeing beyond the words that are often on the papers that we read. So I will, so to speak, "peep" behind that letter that Arthur Lewis wrote to Norman Manley.

The two of them were close friends – they were of the same generation, accomplished scholars from the Caribbean – both of them, in their life, mixing scholarship with social responsibility and doing us, as I have said, a great honour.

When Arthur Lewis received the requests from those who he describes as "prominent Rastas", among whom was Mortimo Planno, he realized an opportunity to affect the society of Jamaica. And before he called on me and Rex Nettleford and Mike Smith, he had already spoken to Norman Manley about the urgency of doing things that mattered to the society of Jamaica in relation to their perception and their belief about the brethren. That does not mean that the report was cooked; it only means that it was *meant to have results*. And one of the questions we have to ask tonight is what *kind* of results it has had.

The second thing I want to bring to your notice is the relationship that Arthur Lewis established with the members of the brethren who wrote him; and it is the relationship of a university to members of the society in which that university lives. Arthur Lewis made it clear that the university would respond to the requests of the brethren *as a university*. That is to say, the help that he would bring would be the help which scholars could bring to a social circumstance. He did not dictate the terms. He asked the brethren who wrote the letter whether they would *accept* this relationship of the brethren and the university.

So the first thing that we did, the three of us *and* the principal, was to meet with the brethren in a primary school in Trench Town where we discussed what we might do, and we asked the brethren whether that was acceptable to them. It was only when we had this agreement that we undertook the study. We spent the next two weeks with the brethren, accumulating information about their life, their condition, their beliefs. Let me remind you of the context in 1960 which caused that letter to be written to the principal, and also caused the principal to take the action he took.

It was the aftermath of Pinnacle. It was the aftermath of Claudius Henry – the Claudius Henry of the disturbances[4] which led to the hanging of one of his men; to the death of men from the police force; to the society's belief that the Rastas were subversive, that they were engaged in preparing, in conjunction with the communists, to upturn the society and to subvert the state. The context, then, was of a time when there was a fervently held belief that the Rastas were a hostile enclave in Jamaican society on the point of radically changing the social order. When the three of us went into what is

Roy Augier

now "the inner city" – the terminology did not exist in 1960 – the police, particularly the officer corps, were hostile to an enterprise which the premier of Jamaica was fully cognizant of and fully supported. That was the context in which the report was written.

I will not go into details of the report, as I indicated in the beginning. I will, instead, skip to the recommendations and read them to you. This is chapter seven of the report – again I regret we do not have it now but we have printed the report and we hope that you will come with enough "Manleys" tomorrow in exchange for the report as well as the other literature that we have provided for you. So I will read as if you had it in your hand. It is chapter seven, the summary of the recommendations: The ten recommendations are as follows:

1. The Government of Jamaica should send a mission to African countries to arrange for the immigration of Jamaicans. Representatives of Rastafari brethren should be included in the mission.
2. Preparations for the mission should be discussed *immediately* with representatives of the Rastafari brethren.
3. The general public should recognize that the great majority of the Rastafari brethren are peaceful citizens, willing to do an honest day's work.
4. The police should complete their security enquiries rapidly and cease to persecute peaceful Rastafari brethren.
5. The building of low-rent houses should be accelerated and provision made for self-help cooperative housing.
6. The government should acquire the principal areas where squatting is now taking place and arrange for water, light, sewage disposal and collection of rubbish.
7. Civic centres should be built with facilities for technical classes, youth clubs, child clinics – the churches and the university shall collaborate.
8. The Ethiopian Orthodox Coptic Church should be invited to establish a branch in West Kingston.
9. Rastafarian brethren should be assisted to establish cooperative workshops.
10. The press and radio facilities should be accorded to leading members of the movement.

I want you to notice what was listed first: "The Government of Jamaica should send a mission to African countries to arrange for the immigration of

Jamaicans"; and second: "Preparations for the mission should be discussed immediately with representatives of the Rastafari brethren".

Arthur Lewis intended the other recommendations, particularly those related to five, six, seven, to be matters that any Jamaican government should be able to find funds for and to insert in their annual budget in the normal way. But the mission, the ceasing of persecution – these are at the top of the list, these were to be immediate.

I look again behind the letter that Arthur Lewis wrote to the premier – he had already agreed with Norman Manley that a number of the brethren should be sent to visit African countries as soon as possible after the premier had received the report. It so happened that I was the only one of the three authors of the report who was able, after we had submitted the report, to follow up, with the premier, the implementation of the first and the second of the recommendations. In the letter, Arthur Lewis had said that, although there was no single leader, he thought the brethren could arrange among themselves a small group of prominent members who would meet with Norman Manley to arrange the group that would go to Africa. As it turned out, this belief of Arthur Lewis was wrong. When Norman Manley attempted to meet "a few prominent Rastas" in the conference room behind his office, which was then in what is now the Ministry of Finance, the room, I can assure you, had more bodies than chairs and more bodies than could fit around the table, because the nature of the brethren, as you know very well, is to think that everyone is a prominent member of the brethren.

Those of you who read the *Gleaner* every day may have noticed in today's section of "This Day in Our Past" an item for 1960, and I will read it to you: "The proposed formal discussion between the premier, the Honourable Norman Manley, QC, and a delegation of Rastafarian representatives is called off as the accredited delegation failed to call at the Premier's office as proposed. Spokesman for the nine-man Rastafarian delegation, Samuel Brown, reports that their plans had suffered a setback through misunderstanding between Mister Manley and themselves." There wasn't a misunderstanding; it was the case that one more group of prominent Rastas was trying to make it to the conference room before the brethren who were already there. As it turned out eventually, Norman Manley, exercising great diplomacy and patience, selected Mortimo Planno, Philmore Alvaranga and Douglas Mack to accompany the other official members of the mission to Africa.

Now, that mission issued two reports – the majority report and the minority report – and I will read my own commentary on those reports for you.

Roy Augier

Let me say that I was surprised, as others were, that Philmore Alvaranga, Douglas Mack and Mortimo Planno wrote a minority report of the mission; and I searched at the time in the text of both of these reports to find the reasons for a minority report, but could find nothing of significance. The minority report was, in some respects, even more detailed and clearly written than the majority report, but there was nothing in it that disagreed with the text of the latter. The majority report, however, had a small and insignificant, but interesting, detail which the minority report did not include. It told how Cecil Gordon and Z. Munroe Scarlett had been baptized into the Ethiopian Orthodox Church by the primate of Ethiopia on 21 April 1961.

But it turned out I was looking in the wrong parts of both reports. The reasons for the minority report were not really to be found in the detailed account of the report where I had looked at first. It was to be found in a paragraph in the majority report's introduction which the minority wished to rebut. I call your attention to it because it is at the heart of the matter of repatriation and is with us still. The majority report had a sentence which I will read verbatim, but in part only: "On almost every occasion it was a point of earnest conversation that centres of exposure of western ideas and customs must tend to modify Jamaicans, and all the black people of the hemisphere, into a way of life dissimilar to the African. Impatience with the African traditions and customs, or too hard a try to bring the African into line would wreck the finest efforts of the scheme." The majority report was here reporting verbatim what they claimed was frequently said to them by the officials of the various African countries they had met. I noted the distinction that when the mission group was in Ethiopia, the emperor, when he met them, had somehow managed to say *both* that Ethiopia would always be open to the people of African origin who lived in the West, and that he hoped, however, that Jamaica would send him the "right sort of people". He spoke to the full delegation in Amharic, but when some of the delegation withdrew, according to the minority report, and only the three members of the Rasta remained – as they were invited to do – they reported that he spoke to them in English. Mortimo and the other two presented him with gifts and he reciprocated. So for the minority report, the response to repatriation by all the African countries visited was always positive and without reservation. I quote now from the minority report which states that the response was "willing – or was universally willing to cooperate in resettling people of African descent within their ancestral borders".

The second difference in the minority report by the Rasta brethren was to assert "our conception of His Imperial Majesty as the messiah. In Ethiopia and in some of the states this conception was not disputed – only in Liberia was there any opposition." In the afternoon of their first day in Ethiopia, they had discussed their belief that the emperor was the returned messiah with the primate of the Ethiopian Orthodox Church. At the end of the discussion, the primate said that perhaps the Bible could be interpreted that way. But, above all, "they likened their meeting with the Emperor to [the] visit of the three wise men who journeyed from the east to visit the baby Jesus". This is a quotation; these are not my words, that is what the minority report said.

Now, one year after this preliminary visit, the government of Jamaica sent three civil servants – Aston Foreman, Wesley Miller and Don Mills – together with Rex Nettleford to the countries that some of the speakers have already referred to: Ghana, Nigeria, Liberia, Sierra Leone and Ethiopia. And that mission, the technical mission, was to lay the foundation for the arrangement of the emigration of Jamaicans to the various countries that were to be visited. This technical mission spent January to March travelling between these five countries, attempting to arrange for the settlement of Jamaicans. However, the arrangements that had been made, the provision of land which had already existed for the settlement in Ethiopia – an arrangement which, as far as I know, exists still – are unlike any other; for in the other countries that were visited – Ghana, Nigeria, Sierra Leone, Liberia – there were no concrete arrangements made for the settlement of Jamaicans.

The land that was set aside by Selassie was for all of the diaspora from the West who wished to settle in Ethiopia; it was not set aside, as someone in the audience shouted, "for Rastas". And as some of you know, the movement of the first people who went there, came not from Jamaica but from the eastern Caribbean. A small number of persons took the emperor's gift and went; and as far as I know it is only some members of the Twelve Tribes from Jamaica who, in due course, using their own initiative, have followed. I have inquired about whether this has continued and have been told that it has not. But when, in a minute or two, I speak to you as a person who lives in Jamaica, who thinks of himself as a Caribbean person, we will think some more about that.

I just want to conclude this part of my talk by saying it is not possible, on the fiftieth anniversary of the 1960 report and the others – the subsequent mission and the technical report – to have a memory of that report without thinking about and possibly commenting, as indeed you will in the next few days, briefly on the effect of that report on the status of the brethren in Jamaica since 1960; and since I am of the academy, I bring to your attention

Roy Augier

also that it is worthwhile our noticing the academic writing about the Rastafari which has followed that report. You will have a chance to peruse this, because we have printed a second set of documents for you of the writings of the last fifty years on the growth of Rastafari and also of its extension out of Jamaica, overseas. I was very pleased to see that the question that I raised concerning the spread of Rastafari will be engaged here: "Why has the Rasta movement expanded not only in the eastern Caribbean but in the New World, in Mexico, in Colombia, in Brazil, the United States and Canada, in Africa, in South Africa, in Europe, in Japan? Why, *why* has this globalization of Rastafarianism taken place?" And I was pleased to see how many of the papers that will be delivered in the coming two days are being delivered by scholars from overseas, giving an account of the existence of Rastafarians in their various countries.

I would like to turn at this point, if I might, to my comrade Barry Chevannes. I was very pleased to be able to "shout-out" and "big-him-up" tonight for the work that he has done, in several articles and in books, to amplify the work that is reported about Rastafarians in our report. Barry, thank you. There is another colleague who I think I saw somewhere in the wings, Ian Boxhill, who has edited a report on the globalization of Rastafari. I don't know whether he will have this on sale, but again I commend this to you. And, finally, but not least, I would like to commend my colleagues in the Institute of Caribbean Studies and the Reggae Studies Unit, which the dean of the faculty has referred to.

So the academic writings about Rastafarianism have been multiple, have been in some of cases profound. I qualify when I say "in some cases" just to speak the truth – they are not all of the same worth, but they are all of some interest.

The more profound, if I might put it this way, question is, "In what respects has the report affected the place of Rastas in Jamaica, the relation between the Rastafarians and the wider society?" I have no doubt that I can say the report was successful in one of its aims. I can speak personally about this. The report effectively reduced the hostility with which the brethren were regarded by society. I want to say also that this was due in no small measure to the brethren themselves, who displayed a great entrepreneurial tendency. Arthur Lewis, because of the nature of the report – its purpose was to inform Jamaican society about the true character of Rastafarians – decided that the report should be sold for nine pence. Some of you are too young to recognize what "nine pennies" meant, but it was practically giving away the report! Some members of the brethren spotted a chance to improve their economic condition. So they came to the Institute of Social and Economic Research, bought the report for nine pence, and then went into Kingston and sold it for five shillings! Of course this meant that we had to reprint the report twice before we understood; we did not recognize the entrepreneurial characteristic until we noticed it was the same brethren who were coming back for the second reprint and the third reprint. Nevertheless, I say this in no spirit of meanness; I do not grudge the profit that was made, because it was their entrepreneurial skill that ensured how widely the report was read.

I can also attest to the number of the middle class who took the opportunity to engage me in conversation, and who would begin by querying the intention of the university in wanting to associate with Rastafarians. And then, in the process of conversation with me, they would admit that they knew one Rastaman personally. That he was an honest Rastaman. That he worked for them, that they could trust him. That he would deal with them in an honest manner. And, gradually, I would say, "Then, if you know one Rastaman who has these qualities, why are you afraid of the others?" And in several of the instances I was very successful in persuading the people – and these were not people I knew, these were people who engaged me in the streets, in the supermarkets, in other places – because they knew that I was associated with the Rastas.

So here I have touched on this very important point of the reduction of the hostility. But I have to qualify it, because the society as a whole was ahead of the police! And tonight we cannot speak about the cessation of the hostility without also remembering Coral Gardens; and also remembering that it took a little while before principals of schools stopped wanting to cut the hair of the children of Rastas before they went to school. (No? It still happens?) Well if they do, I'm sure that you have redress; because one of the effects of the report was for us to get the Ministry of Education to officially instruct principals not to require this measure be taken.

Let us come finally to the questions which I would like to say some words about; some words which I know will not please some of you. But I have the confidence, as I said at the beginning, that in a university where we are accustomed, and entitled, to express our opinion so long as we do it moderately and politely – even if we differ – we should reason together. Let me start with repatriation. We cannot speak about repatriation without attempting to speak about two other words that have profound meaning for us in Jamaican society and to the brethren. And the two other words are Africa and black.

Roy Augier

Let us start with Africa. Africa is geography. In our language, we use the same word to denote a political meaning and a geographical meaning. So we can say "Jamaica" to mean this rock between Negril and St Thomas. And we can use Jamaica to speak about the people who are living in this rock. And we use Africa *in the same way*. That is why I want to bring to your notice the way in which, if we want to assess the effect of the brethren on Jamaican society, we have to speak carefully about these two words.

What the Rastas have undoubtedly done is to bring to the attention of Jamaicans and, in fact, the whole Caribbean that we have roots on the other side of the Atlantic; that we have roots in Africa: Africa as geography, Africa as culture and therefore Africa as history. Many of us, and that includes people with *all kinds of complexions*, were brought up to think of roots only out of the side of the Atlantic that we call "Europe". Without the benefit of association with Freddie Hickling or Leachim Semaj,[5] I had worked out for myself that the denial of roots in Africa had a bad effect on our psyche, on our persons, on our beings.

I have a concept which is not mine – I did not invent it, but I like to think of all of us as being *whole*. And if we are not whole, then we are broken, we are fractured, and being *fractured* means that we are not at ease with ourselves. There is a phrase which I find very useful. It says, "A person is happy in his or her own skin", and that for me is true, irrespective of the colour of that skin. It seemed to me that I was of a generation in which an education had been provided, in all its ramifications – not simply in the classroom – which involved a denial of the African roots. For me that meant, therefore, that our personality was fractured. I formed this conclusion before I had met any Rastas – in fact, before I had left St Lucia. And I must tell you that when I came to Jamaica in 1954, I came practically straight from the university in England – I did not go back to St Lucia, I came to Jamaica, to this land here, at Mona. From the day I landed I felt, indeed I knew, that I was in the Caribbean. I was at home. And for not one moment since 1954 have I not felt at home in Jamaica.

And it is about home that I want to speak to you! I want to ask you (the Rastafari) to help me to find the essential truth, the essential truths, in that belief or in those beliefs; and I do not say this in a sense of disparagement of your beliefs. I take the chance of saying to you that what I get from the central tenet of your religion is that when we make a physical representation in our Christian churches of the person of the God that became man, we should represent that man as we ourselves look. I still find it a pity that, in so

You Must Be Willing to Reason Together

many Christian churches of all denominations, Christ or Jesus is represented as a European, as a white man. This, for me, is one of the ways I measured the effect of the brethren upon the society. You may not like what I am saying here, but I believe that you are not behaving in a way in which you are the least of the society.[6] You need somehow to make the case for the representation of the man/God in the image of ourselves.

One of the ways in which I seek to understand repatriation is to understand the positive; to understand it as your longing for converting Jamaica into a true homeland. Let me make some remarks again which some of you may find offensive but which are not meant to be. There is an element which runs through the whole of our society – for those who inhabit the hillsides, to those who inhabit the lower ends near the harbour – and it is a dependency upon the outsiders; a dependency that is seen in the way in which the tourist trade, which is important to us, is presented. I cannot drive to the airport without thinking of the way in which those persons, who have political responsibility, as well as ourselves, have taken no pride in the city in which we live.

It is impossible for me to drive without thinking that we cannot even keep the bush in the central roadway of that passage to Rockfort, to the Harbour View corner, tidy – not to speak of the rest of Kingston. Now, not to do it ourselves is dependency. To speak, as some of the speakers tonight have done, about the wherewithal for repatriation coming from abroad is misguided – it will never happen.

And I will take the opportunity to tell you that when Mortimo came back from the mission, he knew that repatriation could not happen in the way in which he did expect it to. And in coming to that knowledge, he was fulfilling Arthur Lewis's intention for the brethren to have first-hand knowledge of Ghana, Nigeria, Sierra Leone and Liberia, and to recognize that other meaning of Africa: the politics of Africa. And to know that – no matter what Garvey had dreamt of, no matter what you, in the brethren, dream of – these countries would not, and they have not, made any provision to accommodate you.

So I say to you, why look for the homeland? There is work *here*. Why not turn Jamaica into a homeland? What Arthur Lewis wanted you to have was this knowledge of Africa so that our roots in Africa could be properly understood. The roots of Africa are part of our history, part of our culture, part of our personality. I promise you that I am not being disparaging when I say to you that our future lies in understanding our relationship with the culture, the

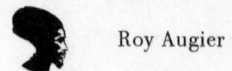

Roy Augier

politics of Africa – with its history and its present condition. You as brethren have a mission in that respect.

Think of what has actually happened among you. Those of you who have grasped the true relation of the Rasta to Africa have liberated themselves. They are the ones whose economic condition is several times better than yours. They are the ones who have taken the music, who have taken the culture, who tour, who go to Japan, who make money in Africa, who make money in the United States. Why do they do it? They do it with your culture. If you want a source of economic independence, you have to follow in their footsteps; you have to deal with Babylon.

When you celebrate Bob Marley, when you celebrate the others, are you not celebrating a Rasta who has made his life in acknowledgement of Babylon? You cannot efface Babylon. I therefore want to end tonight by saying to you, that if you care for a continuing relationship with the university, then you must enter into the relationship Arthur Lewis asked of the brethren in 1960. You must be willing to reason together.

Acknowledgements

This chapter was originally presented as the opening address of the inaugural Rastafari Studies Conference in 2010.

Notes

1. Within the Rastafari movement there is a propensity for word play – or morpho-semantic manipulation to derive new meanings and to get at the core interpretation based on demonstration of purpose. With this in mind, the acronym for the University College of the West Indies – commonly called by the rest of the society by the acronym "UC", was critiqued by Rastafari as "U-blind".
2. Jamaica was not yet independent and Norman Manley was, therefore, not the prime minister but the premier of the country.
3. University College of the West Indies, now the University of the West Indies.
4. Pinnacle the first Rastafari encampment established in the 1940s by Leonard Howell was destroyed by the governmental authoritiy in 1954. In 1960

a self-anointed holy man, the Reverend Claudius Henry, RB (for "Repairer of the Breach") stirred an estimated twenty thousand bearded cultists into a back-to-Africa frenzy and caused great scrutiny to emerge around the movement as a plot to overthrow the Jamaican government was unearthed within his organization. This was considered an important consideration in the cry from within Rastafari for justice and particularly repatriation as they felt victimized by the Jamaican society – that had vilified the movement over the last decade of the 1950s.

5. Freddie Hickling and Leachim Semaj are Jamaican psychologists who have commented on the impact of colonialism on the Jamaican psyche.

6. Augier starts out with the disclaimer of saying that which the Rastafari brethren would perhaps not like to hear, and adds in the same breath that the Rastafari are behaving like the "least of the society", as if to suggest that the movement has yet to take its rightful and elevated place in society.

Chapter 4

When Goldilocks Met the Dreadlocks
Reflections on the Contributions of Carole D. Yawney to Rastafari Studies

John Homiak

Both *a yard* and *abraad*, the 1970s was a pivotal and momentous decade for Jamaica. There was the election of Michael Manley as prime minister in 1972; he was ushered into office through an association with Rastafari symbols and anti-imperialist sentiments. The idea that delegations of Rastafari elders could gain unprecedented access to houses of government became increasingly disturbing to the ranks of middle-class and elite Jamaicans – even as some of their own sons and daughters began to embrace new versions of Rastafari. Fear of "dread at the controls", coupled with Manley's socialist policies and pro-Castro stance led to their increasing flight to Miami. The table for these developments had been set by the historic state visit of Emperor Haile Selassie I to Jamaica in 1966 and the banning of pan-African scholar Walter Rodney from the island in 1968. Rodney's banning led to riots in Kingston that radicalized many Jamaican and Caribbean students enrolled at the University College of the West Indies where he had been an instructor. Rastafari found common cause with the politics of the Black Power movement, ushering in Jamaica's first truly postcolonial decade.

Beyond the shores of the island the sounds of reggae music – especially the anthems of Marley, Tosh and Burning Spear – echoed across college campuses in North America and Europe and could be heard in urban clubs and dancehalls. The Vietnam War had not yet ended. Martin Luther King and Robert Kennedy had been assassinated as the Civil Rights movement rolled on; Watergate, the invasion of Cambodia and My Lai were yet to come and

When Goldilocks Met the Dreadlocks

opposition to apartheid in South Africa was on the rise. The musical poetry and protest messages of reggae appealed to the poor, and to alienated middle-class youth disenchanted with the hypocrisy of the system and looking beyond the empty materialism of their parents.

All of this – coupled with the local trials and tribulations of the *sufferah* class – served as grist for a compelling Rastafari political and cultural critique of the international order. Using reggae as their principal vehicle, the sons and daughters of Jah had resurrected Garvey's vision of a globally imagined black community with themselves at its centre. For many, there was near-biblical certainty that a day of dread reckoning must come to redress the historical injustices of slavery and the continued exploitation of black people. This expectation was so high that on 7 July 1977 – the day when "two sevens clashed" (as Joseph Hill's now legendary song of that title would have it) – schoolchildren across Kingston stayed home waiting for the dreaded apocalyptic event to unfold (Jahlani Niaah, personal communication, 2011).

Into this zeitgeist stepped a young white Canadian graduate student in anthropology named Carole Diane Yawney. Of Ukrainian descent, diminutive, with fair complexion, straight blonde hair and blue eyes, this "Goldilocks"

Figure 4.1a. Carole Yawney, Palisadoes, 1970

Figure 4.1b. Mortimo Planno, Sidewalk University, 1970

57

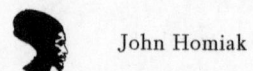

John Homiak

seemed an unlikely participant in the life of the ad hoc communities that Rastafari had cobbled together in the "dread wastelands" of West Kingston.[1] Over the next few years, however, she would establish a long-term commitment to Rastafari ethnography that would evolve in collaboration with Ras Mortimo Planno, one of the movement's most historic figures.

Her intensive and scrupulously principled fieldwork would result in what is arguably some of the most intimate and insightful understandings about the cultural and spiritual life of the Rastafari yet written. The long-term nature of her fieldwork is also of note because it afforded Carole a deeper knowledge of the Rastafari and of the diversity within their ranks as well as a basis to discern changes in the culture that occurred over periods of time beyond the typical eighteen to twenty-four months of dissertation fieldwork (see Taggart and Sandstrom 2011, 2). In the course of her work Carole Yawney would also produce an unparalleled archive of field notes, photographs, correspondence, recordings and collectibles that bore witness to this critical period in the movement's development. Not only would Carole document many of the now legendary people, places and events in the history of the movement, she would later pioneer research on the forefront of its globalizing impulse.[2]

Despite her long-term commitment to Rastafari ethnography, the work of Carole Yawney is not well appreciated outside of those scholars who work on the movement. She intentionally chose, for whatever reasons, to publish in obscure journals, magazines and ephemera (see Yawney 1979, 1981, 1983a, 1983b, 1984). While she produced a number of exceptionally insightful articles and book chapters, Carole never completed a monograph-length publication. At the time of her passing in 2005 she was still working on a book entitled "In a Government Yard in Trench Town: The Rastafari Renaissance of the 1970s". The fact that this work was never published reflected, I believe, Carole's own struggle with closure on relationships within the Rastafari community that had become an inextricable part of her life. In pointing this out, I write both as a colleague and close personal friend. More to the point, Carole Yawney and I were research partners during the last fifteen years of her life. We both had similar immersions into Rastafari, she beginning in the 1970s and me in the 1980s. We shared notes, thoughts and ideas on almost a daily basis and continued to work with Rastafari both in Jamaica and internationally.[3]

In this chapter I reflect on the contributions of Carole Yawney to what has become known as "Rastafari studies". Carole herself never sought to explicitly define such a field. But because she was first and foremost an ethnographer, she was clear on issues of methodology that might usefully shape this area of study. The first is that the scale, complexity and diversity of the movement are such that it calls for researchers to locate themselves and their observations within the decentralized and dynamic sociology of the movement. Perhaps because there are so few ethnographers of Rastafari, this kind of critical positioning is rarely found in the extant literature. Even in Jamaica during the early 1970s, Rastafari had become too organizationally complex and ideologically dynamic for any one researcher, or even any single Rastafari participant, to grasp in its fullness. While allowing for eclectic methods, Carole argued that significant scholarly contributions to understanding the movement required a critical and reflexive positioning through which a researcher defined his or her social location vis-à-vis the larger complexity of Rastafari. By this she meant being explicit about how one worked with Rastafari. This included specifying one's methods (for example, interviews, surveys and/or participant-observation; or community studies as opposed to network analysis). It also meant being explicit about how and with whom one developed relationships and acquired information on/knowledge of Rastafari. The latter presumes an appreciation of the fact that Rastafari subjects develop their own social locations within the movement. And it also means giving attention to how factors such as race, class and gender influenced one's relationships and understandings (see Yawney 2002, 134).

    Of her early ethnography in Jamaica, it should be noted that Carole's research served to prefigure the limitations inherent in fieldwork's localizing strategies. This reflected the decentralized and shifting demography of Rastafari, one that involved an oscillation between rural and urban contexts as a primary dynamic in the development of the movement (see Homiak 1996, 788; Post 1981, 188–89). Although Carole took up residence in West Kingston in 1970–71, she was a mobile ethnographer who came to appreciate the reach and fluidity of Rastafari connections across the island. In addition, her primary collaborators maintained active relationships outside Jamaica, not the least of which included their political links to members of the Rastafari settler community in Ethiopia. As her research came to focus increasingly on the global aspects of the movement, Carole argued for multi-sited or multi-centred approaches inasmuch as one could study Rastafari in Brooklyn or London as well as Jamaica. She also repeatedly emphasized that Rastafari in its contemporary global context has given rise to a plethora of cultural expressions and is now exponentially more complex than its Jamaican incarnation (Yawney 1985a, 1985b, 1995,

John Homiak

1999, 2004). For her, Rastafari in the global context was simultaneously a theocratic/patriarchal/popular culture, a "global imaginary", a transnational social movement, an expression of pan-Africanism and a form of, in James Clifford's words, "travelling culture" (1992). For Carole this meant that scholars researching the movement in the international sphere could not privilege any single interpretive perspective.

It is clear that Carole's own appreciation of Rastafari was shaped not only by factors of race, class and gender, but by the particular networks of Rastafari with whom she initially engaged, the long-term, intensive and "initiatory" character of her ethnographic work, and the strategic relationships she maintained with significant brethren and sistren. All of this spanned a period of thirty-five years both in Jamaica and internationally. Her own critical ethnographic methods draw our attention to the nature of the insights she produced about the culture of Rastafari as well as raise critical questions about the different ways in which researchers (of whatever disciplinary persuasions) have come to produce "knowledge" about the Rastafari from local and global perspectives. In Carole's case, her contributions were inseparable from the lifelong relationship and extraordinary collaboration she developed with Ras Mortimo Planno, arguably the movement's leading figure from the late 1950s through much of the 1990s. To date, their collaboration arguably stands as the single most productive relationship between a Rastafari leader and a non-Rastafari "outsider" of any background. As will become clear below, Carole's relationship with Mortimo was central to the social location she developed within the movement, and indirectly facilitated and informed much of the work she did with the Rastafari later in Jamaica and elsewhere. The longevity of their relationship also made Carole a singular ethnographic "witness" to life in the legendary camps and yards of West Kingston. It is of note that during this incredibly vibrant and dynamic period of Rastafari development in the 1970s, she created a documentary record of Mortimo's public speeches and reasonings that were missed or ignored by both the Jamaican media as well as local scholars.[4]

The extended duration of Carole Yawney's ethnographic work is also notable for the profound changes in the cultural expressions, diversity and complexity of the movement that she witnessed in Jamaica and internationally. We should appreciate as well that Carole – as the ethnographic "instrument" – also changed over this same period of time. Her published articles and archival data and materials should be seen as a baseline from which to assess how Rastafari–researcher engagements have changed and developed over the years. As a white female Canadian, Carole consistently emphasized the view that "moving with Rastafari" (meaning being allowed to participate in their inner community life) was a privilege that could not be taken for granted and one that should be subject to ongoing critical review. If for no other reason, her work warrants consideration in terms of what it reveals about the shifting and often contentious politics of representation surrounding a predominantly black liberation movement. This was something to which she, as a white non-Rastafari academic, was always acutely sensitive.

Notes on an Evolving Rastafari Scholarship

> Why yuh talk 'bout research? Research! No, is an I-search. The mon haffi search himself first. An' yuh cyaan study Rastafari. Mi say, no mon can study Rastafari. Yuh can only live Rastafari!
> – Bongo Watto 1983, Bull Bay, St Thomas, Jamaica

Carole Yawney's seminal (or what she from her womanist perspective might term "ovarian") contributions to Rastafari studies need to be appreciated in terms of what little was known about Rastafari at the end of the 1960s. At the time of her initial fieldwork in 1970 there had been virtually no ethnographic research on the Rastafari – if by this we mean a situation in which the ethnographer/researcher is actually living among the brethren and sistren, and participating with them in the flow of their everyday domestic and ritual lives. This was hardly surprising since the camps and yards where the largely disenfranchised members of the movement had come to congregate by this time were defined as spaces virtually off-limits to most "respectable" Jamaicans. Despite this fact, some Rastafari already had limited experience with several researchers. Two of these, George E. Simpson and Sheila Kitzinger, had more or less stumbled upon the Rastafari presence in West Kingston while pursuing research on other concerns (see Simpson 1955a, 1955b; Kitzinger 1969). Neither of them, however, had any linguistic competence in patois or Jamaican English. Leonard Barrett, a Jamaican working in the area of the sociology of religion, brokered his own connections to the Rastafari through sympathetic clergy familiar with several "leaders" of the movement and gathered information primarily through interviews that were arranged by appointment, rather than through intensive participant-observation (Barrett 1969).

John Homiak

The most politically important early research on the movement was the publication *Report on the Rastafari Movement in Kingston, Jamaica* (Smith, Augier and Nettleford 1960). The report was the result of an intervention made by various Rastafari leaders to the University of the West Indies to address the deterioration of relations between the Rastafari and the wider society since the mid-1950s. It is held by most accounts that in 1960 Ras Mortimo Planno approached Dr Arthur Lewis, the then chancellor of the university, and petitioned him to conduct a study of the movement in order to correct the many public misconceptions that had been spread about the Rastafari as revolutionaries and criminals. The report was described by one of the principals of the study, Rex Nettleford, as a "rapid survey", the object of which was to collect information on the doctrines, history, organization and needs of the movement (Nettleford 1972, 52–53). Despite the importance of this publication, it is fair to say the literature on the Rastafari remained quite thin at the end of the 1960s.

What was available at the time would have provided little guidance to a prospective researcher with regard to how she or he might actually proceed with an in-depth field study. It was, accordingly, more or less entirely up to Carole Yawney to develop her own field methods and to define for herself the research "community" within which she would work. It should be noted that Carole was not alone in her interest in the movement, as the early 1970s marked the beginning of more intensive research on the movement. Other students of the movement included Father Joseph Owens, a white American-born Jesuit priest, who had been working for the Social Action Centre in St Andrew and was interested in demonstrating the breadth and theological coherence of Rastafari thought. There was also [the late] Barry Chevannes who, in exploring the origins of Rastafari, became interested in its continuities with African-Jamaican Christianity (Revival), the culture of the peasantry, and its relevance to Jamaican nationhood. These three scholars – Yawney, Owens and Chevannes – all worked with rather different methods and each defined, and no doubt experienced, their fieldwork in quite different ways. This reflects the fact that "the field" does not exist in any objective or natural sense but rather is constructed through particular social relationships, and the ways in which these relationships are initiated, developed and embodied in relation to the interests of the researcher (see Clifford 1992, 69–88).[5]

Carole maintained that the brethren had evolved a more or less consistent approach to researchers by the time of her initial fieldwork in 1970 – one that was critical and guarded, if not actively hostile. I think it can be argued that this general orientation prevailed through the 1980s and, in some quarters of the movement, into the 1990s. Typically the Rastafari identified researchers as denizens of the citadels of Babylon, and consigned them to the categories of spies, members of the CIA and "pirates", or dubbed them "scribes and Pharisees" who functioned to relay information back to the centres of Babylonian control. As members of a traditionally fugitive culture that had collectively suffered at the hands of the colonial and postcolonial state, the Rastafari had an understandable interest in developing their own strategies for controlling researchers by limiting access their to their yards and camps and the cultural spaces over which they exercised jurisdictional control. This process of control went hand in hand with sustaining the protocols of cultural intimacy by which the Rastafari maintained both an identity and a sense of community.[6]

Given the "Rastacizing" of Jamaica over the past four decades, it is sometimes difficult to appreciate the fact that many Jamaicans regarded members of the movement as criminals or dismissed them as ganja-soaked louts and fanatics at the outset of the 1970s.[7] Many others regarded the Rastafari as unpatriotic and anti-Jamaica because of their asserted Ethiopian identity and the stance they took on repatriation. Prior to this, the first-generation leaders of Rastafari were charged with sedition and/or placed in the mental asylum for their beliefs (see Hoenisch 1988). All of this serves to remind us that the movement was forged, and continues to develop, within a politically charged field of relations shaped by force, power and counter-hegemonic resistance. Insufficient attention has been given to how researchers have dealt with these factors and how they have limited or shaped access to, and rapport with, Rastafari subjects.

For the most part, the literature remains ethnographically naïve about concerns that are now widely appreciated in critical and postcolonial studies. This would include issues such as how power and privilege have shaped not only the construction of scholarly discourse *about* the movement but the production of discourse *within* the movement in terms of the contending voices that structure its polycephalous social organization. But both in scholarly and participant discourses, the issue of whether (and how) cultural meanings (for example, repatriation, gender equality) do or do not get talked about remains a politically situated one. Rastafari scholarship, in Carole's view, was still coming to terms with such concerns; and earlier studies, she felt, had not fully addressed the fact that disciplinary canons themselves shaped or limited how a movement like Rastafari is represented (see Polier and Roseberry 1989, 245–64).

John Homiak

In this regard it is worth revisiting the fact that, in the early 1970s, prevailing anthropological and sociological concepts had not evolved much beyond pigeon-holing the movement as a millenarian or messianic "cult" (see Simpson 1955a; Patterson 1964; Barrett 1969, 15–17; Kitzinger 1969; Nettleford 1972, 42–45). In the academy, phenomena labelled in this way tended to be reduced to aberrations created by social upheavals or to be seen as ephemeral forms of proto-political agency. A semiotic concept of culture – one that focused on the understanding of socially meaningful action – had not yet come into vogue; and structural-functional approaches to these phenomena either reduced them to external sociopolitical factors or grounded analysis in the presumed falsity of their belief systems. This tended to foreclose deeper inquiry into how the subjects of research actually experienced their world or how their worldviews might support a process of meaning-making that shaped communal lives and cultural practices (see Patterson 1964; Barrett 1969, 15–16; cf. Burridge 1969, 122–30). Scholars who sought to explore and sympathetically present such movements typically had to deal with the attendant negative publicity and with being cast in the role as apologists for whatever *logos* constituted the system of thought under scrutiny. This was certainly true for scholars of Rastafari in the early years (Barrett 1969, 1; personal communication, George Simpson 1996).[8]

Rastafari also presented the additional challenge of attempting to make sense of a phenomenon that was manifestly "religious" – inasmuch as its adherents articulated "ultimate sacred postulates" (Rappaport 1979), addressed "the really real" (Geertz 1973) and sought to uphold a transcendental framework (Yawney 1979) – yet whose participants emphatically rejected the idea that their way of life constituted a "religion". This was the challenge of theorizing the complex of Rastafari practices referred to as *livity*, essentially a theocratic concept of culture (meaning one in which adherents recognized divine agency as permeating all aspects of thought and behavior). It may well be the case that the term "livity" had not acquired currency until the 1970s; the term is not referred to by Simpson (1955a, 1955b), Barrett (1969) or the authors of the report. Carole Yawney's in-depth work of cultural analysis brought this concept to the surface in relation to her interest in understanding the dynamics of Rastafari as a spiritual and interpretive community. In her work, livity is situated at the heart of the quest to create an all-encompassing fabric of meanings that supports a transcendental framework oriented to the divine (Yawney 1979). It is this framework, defined by the paradigmatic contrast between the domains of Zion and Babylon, that upholds the identity of the Rastafari as permanent liminars[9] – individuals who, while physically contained in Babylon, remain spiritually free in Zion.

From the time I first met her in the early 1980s, Carole had been arguing that the burgeoning literature on Rastafari itself needed to be deconstructed from a sociology of knowledge perspective – that is, not only how the identity and location of different researchers influence how and what they know of Rastafari, but how "knowledge" of Rastafari is influenced by prevailing political issues and the shifting concerns and perspectives of the participants themselves within the movement. All of this made sense within the context of a polycephalous social movement where some voices clamour for expression more than others. Given the fact that intensive scholarship on Rastafari did not actually begin until the early 1970s, the different researcher reactions to the millenarian, messianic and "cult" concepts applied to the movement are perhaps of note.

Rex Nettleford and Barry Chevannes, while acknowledging the salience of millenarian ideation within Rastafari thought, tended to downplay the definitive nature of such labelling by emphasizing the historical context within which the movement was set and the contested regimes of value at play within Jamaica as a plural society. It can be argued that their project has been to show the many ways in which Rastafari religiosity and its culture are organically Jamaican and have influenced the views of the wider society. For Chevannes, this underscored links to the worldview of Revival and to that of the Jamaican peasantry. While each endorsed the Rastafari critique of the wider society and saluted the movement's valorization of Jamaica's African heritage, it is probably also fair to say that both regarded the actual politics of physical repatriation as problematic. From this perspective, it is difficult to see their scholarship as other than a national (or perhaps regional) project. By contrast, I would argue that Yawney – who as a Canadian had no vested connection to Jamaica – broke in a fundamentally different way with the limitations of millenarian studies in developing her own perspective on the movement. Her initiation by Mortimo Planno into sessions of reasoning gave her first-hand insight into the social context in which ideology was reproduced and led her to posit Rastafari as a kind of "popular front" that was evolving in dialogue with the wider society. Through this experience, she came to recognize the movement as an interpretive community and an anti-colonial black vanguard capable of producing an ongoing critique not only of postcolonial Jamaican society but of the dominant world system as well (see Yawney 1976; Owens 1976, 160). It could be argued that her most salient operative framework was not one of continuity with African-Jamaican culture or of exposing the inherent Jamaicanness of the movement, but of locating Rastafari (wherever it may emerge) within a pan-African and black internationalist perspective. Nettleford and Chevannes, of course, did this as well by situating Rastafari in the context of Garveyism and Ethiopianism, but the point I am making should be taken as one of relative emphasis.

Whereas Nettleford and Chevannes developed a view of the movement based primary on an experience of the Jamaican context, I believe that Yawney can be seen as fashioning an internationalist perspective quite early in her work. Given Mortimo Planno's status as a black internationalist, this was hardly by accident. In the environs of West Kingston – in places like Trench Town, Foreshore Road, Dungle, Redemption Ground and Grass Yard – Mortimo introduced her to visitors from North America, Guyana, Trinidad and Nigeria among other places. This reflected the active connections that Mortimo maintained with Ethiopian World Federation Local 1 in New York City and his connections with federation locals in London, and brethren like Jah Bones and others who had migrated to England in the second half of the 1950s (see Jah Bones 1985).[10] Carole accordingly understood that the Rastafari sanctuaries in Kingston to which she gained access were already internationally networked sites. She learned of the visit by Miriam Makeba and Stokely Carmichael to Back-o-Wall in 1963 and visits by Walter Rodney and Maurice Bishop to camps and yards in West Kingston later in that decade.[11] During her initial fieldwork Carole met Professor Ephraim Isaac, a lecturer in Ethiopian history and religion at Harvard, who was invited by Mortimo as the head of Local 37 of the Ethiopian World Federation to attend events in Jamaica surrounding the celebration of All-Africa Day (May 1971). It was Professor Isaac who later sent Amharic language tapes to Mortimo to mount his Amharic language training in West Kingston (see Yawney 1999). And of course she was aware of the international travel of reggae ambassadors like Bob Marley, Peter Tosh and Jimmy Cliff, and their link to Planno's gates in the early 1970s and before. As an international ambassador for the movement, Mortimo himself was part of this pattern of international communication, travel and exchanges. Carole came to appreciate all of this quite early in her movements with Rastafari. She was, after all, the first person to greet Mortimo in 1972 when he landed at LaGuardia Airport in New York on his return from his second trip to Africa.

For Carole, all of this problematized a place-oriented concept of culture and/or community. These concerns also begged the anthropological question of how Rastafari should be "imagined" as a community or even how its formative history and parameters should be mapped (Yawney and Homiak 1999; Gilroy 1993, 227). In this regard, I believe it is telling that Carole came to define herself vis-à-vis the movement through the phrase "If Rastafari is for Africa, I am for Rastafari". This mantra clearly reflected the politics of her mentor, Mortimo Planno, whose pan-African position and teachings on repatriation are well known. But I believe it also reflected the strong internationalist currents that she encountered in her own ethnographic experience, starting with her initial work in Trench Town.

It is thus perhaps unsurprising that Carole began to collapse the boundary between "the field" (meaning Rastafari in Jamaica) and "home" (her university; residence) almost immediately following her initial eighteen months of fieldwork.[12] Carole brought Mortimo to Toronto several times during the 1970s, along with some of his associates and, later, other Rastafari elders including Ras Sam Brown and Ras Iration I. She became involved in organizing the first international gathering of Rastafari in Toronto in 1982, and in assisting elders from Jamaica and elsewhere to travel internationally in 1984 and 1986. Working in this manner, Carole was enabling part of the very phenomenon that she was studying.

Based on this and other factors I would argue that Carole Yawney's Rastafari ethnography was *prematurely postmodern* – a characterization that she would almost surely dismiss.[13] I use the description here because both Carole and I felt that the movement was, in certain ways, international from its genesis and prefigured a postmodern geography of identity that exists *here* and *there* simultaneously (Bammer 1994, xii). In addition, description and analysis also pose certain challenges to traditional anthropological concepts that are normative, bounded and/or structural in nature. By this I mean to say that Rastafari, through its extreme multivocality and diffuse spatiality, complicates both the location of the researcher and participants as well as their respective representational authority. Through its distinc-

Peter Tosh

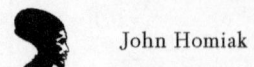
John Homiak

tive way of knowing, it has re-centred a black self and an African history, contesting the master narratives of European history; and in its dynamic fluidity it routinely "confounds the wise and prudent" by defying any precise location or specification. Mortimo Planno and others have applied the oxymoronic label of "the modern antique" to Rastafari – a reference that, if fully unpacked, would launch a dissertation. Suffice it to say here that this phrase describes a movement/message that emerged not simply in response to the historical circumstances of a single modern place (Jamaica), but from a confluence of events elsewhere in an ancient empire (Ethiopia) that radiated globally and transcended space in terms of how this movement/message resonated with the wider diasporic condition of African peoples. Carole understood that Rastafari would require a new vocabulary and a new set of methodologies if it were to be described and interpreted at even the most modestly adequate levels.

Defining a Research Community: "In a Government Yard in Trench Town"

Truly, there are many mansions within Fadda's House, seen? But wi find [that] there der is now nuff "versions" and "de-versions" within I-n-I culture that develop since His Imperial Majesty come here in 1966. That mean to show that mon really haffi know which part 'im stand.
– Bongo Poro [Nyahbinghi patriarch] 1983, Bull Bay, St Thomas, Jamaica

Carole Yawney arrived in Jamaica at the beginning of January 1970 as a graduate student from McGill University in Montreal, Canada. She had never been to Jamaica before, so she was literally "coming in from the cold". At the time she knew only one person – the head of the Department of Psychiatry at the University Hospital – a colleague of her thesis advisor. She had also been given the names of two Rastafari brethren by her advisor at McGill, one of which had been passed on by another psychiatrist from Montreal who, the year before, had given a paper about Rastafari at a major conference in Jamaica. Her initial plan was to survey the urban scene to gain a sense of the range of Rastafari expressions and activities that might be open to her. Scouring the local papers she found room and board in a tenement yard in Central Kingston where she resided for the first few months of her sojourn.

For the first few weeks she followed up introductions from people who put her in contact with Rastafari individuals or groups, thus seeking to gain a sense of the range of Rastafari expressions and orientations. One day, by chance, she met the minister of finance who also happened to be the Jamaica Labour Party's member of parliament for West Kingston. This was Edward Seaga, a Harvard-educated sociologist-turned-politician. In her meeting with him, Yawney proposed West Kingston, perhaps Trench Town, as her field site. Seaga dissuaded her, at first, politely, noting several locations she should be careful to avoid including Salt Lane and Dungle. By the time her meeting ended the message was clear: West Kingston was out of the question. There was absolutely no way she could work in his area. It was too dangerous; certainly too dangerous for a woman. She would have to find something else.

In the meantime she was determined to follow up the name of a Rastafari that the Montreal psychiatrist had passed to her thesis advisor. The name was Mortimo Planno. It immediately became clear that Planno was a major Jamaican personality known by Rastafari and non-Rastafari alike. He was arguably the most famous Rastaman on the island. Just a few years earlier it was Planno who had disembarked Emperor Haile Selassie from his plane at Palisadoes and there was a recollection that he had been one of three Rastafari sent to Ethiopia by the Jamaican government in 1960. This all sounded promising. A few days later, with the help of her university contact, Carole managed to find Planno's yard at 18 Fifth Street in Trench Town. With her contact, she made her way to the back of a yard that housed some ten families. There, eight or nine brethren were engaged in a reasoning as the chalice passed among them. Yawney's initial encounter with Planno did not go well. She reported:

> [Planno] didn't make any effort to reason with me, although he had made several pronouncements in a loud voice to the yard at large about decadent hippies and CIA spies. And he made it clear that he regarded my appearance [in his yard] as part of a conspiracy involving Rasta. I learned for the first time that the psychiatrist from Montreal who had set me upon his trail had given a paper the previous year in Jamaica at a major professional conference about Rastafari as a benign but *delusional belief system*. [. . .] Planno regarded my association with psychiatrists with a great deal of suspicion. We hung around for a while until we learned that he had left the yard altogether without saying goodbye. (Yawney 1985a, 7)[14]

John Homiak

While keeping an eye open for other possibilities, she routinely visited Planno's yard for the next three months and engaged with the brethren there. It was during this time that she came to understand how the Rastafari, particularly Dreadlocks Rastafari, managed to "screen off" and "control" researchers without actually having to effect their physical exclusion. The first line of defence was the use of an arcane argot that recast an already challenging Jamaican English (at least for standard English speakers and other foreigners) in its own unique dynamic code. This speech form was part of a specifically Dreadlocks Rastafari innovation (see Yawney 1979; Homiak 1995; Pollard 1994). As is now common knowledge, the cohort of Dreadlocks Rastafari that became ascendant across the cultural geography of Rastafari during the mid-1960s was associated with an intense burning spiritual zeal and became known for their contentious and fiery dispositions. Outsiders and researchers soon learned that this zeal could be deployed for the purpose of policing the boundaries of community resulting in significant challenges to the researcher (see, for example, Chevannes 1994, 209–11; Homiak 1999, 95–99). Along these lines, Yawney has written that the brethren "will offer a copious amount of ganja to smoke to study its effects and to interview the researcher under its influence. Rastafari also engage visitors in *strenuous* dialogues in an effort to tease out any hidden agendas or assumptions [and] if the researcher is not prepared to participate without reservation, it can be an uncomfortable experience" (Yawney 1999, 162).

It must be pointed out that Carole's bloodless and matter-of-fact description above is a carefully crafted understatement. It sets aside the often dramatic agonistics associated with how the brethren manage social boundaries around their backstage. As I know from my own experience (and my many discussions with Carole about her experiences), Rastafari and non-Rastafari alike were invariably more than suspicious of a white researcher who suddenly appears in their midst. The tests that follow are by no means simply singular once-and-for all events that the researcher either definitively passes or fails. Rather, the ethnographer seeking to "move with" the brethren or sistren within their own sanctuaries is made to conform to their imperatives and is subject to what can only be described as an extended probationary period. Closure of this period may, in fact, never come.[15] Carole found herself under intense continuous scrutiny in Mortimo's yard and in other yards to which he and his brethren were linked. These included Skipper's yard in Salt Lane, the Dungle and its Temple, and the Coal Yard, all legendary sites in West Kingston, as well as Brother Wallace's yard in Seven

When Goldilocks Met the Dreadlocks

Mile, Brother Dessi's yard in St Ann and various other sites around the island. Within certain limits, any brethren who might "come on to the yard" (arrive in the yard) could reinitiate a test or an interrogation if she was present. Was she a spy, a druggler (i.e., someone who is a drug smuggler—hustling drugs for a living), an agent-provocateur, a communist, a hippy or just a hapless fool?

For Carole there were months of tests and ordeals that involved such things as interminable biblical harangues that likened researchers to "scribes and Pharisees", pirates, spies, or the CIA. She endured fierce "nose-end reasonings" that invaded her personal space and that were intended to intimidate, confuse and to determine if she was a "weak-heart".[16] And, as she has pointed out, there were extensive sessions of smoking the ritual herbs

Figure 4.2a. Dungle Wall, festival preparations, 1970

71

John Homiak

Figure 4.2b. Coal Yard near Salt Lane, West Kingston, 1970

pipe or "chalice" intended to "blaak up" the researcher (meaning disorient them with ganja) and/or to determine both her psychological resilience and the nature of her "consciousness". She was made to endure long tirades of biblical intensity that critiqued her as a representative of the Babylonian world and she was expected to respond as if it all made sense. All manner of ploys were used to disrupt or destabilize expectations of normal social interaction.[17] These probationary controls served as a prelude to initiation with all of the classic features of liminal instability, uncertainty and resocialization.

Undaunted, she pressed on. She quickly came to realize that Mortimo and the activities in his yard were special. His address on Fifth Street was arguably *the* centre of Rastafari activity in West Kingston with something on the order of thirty to thirty-five brethren coming through the yard every day. But during these early months, at no time during these visits did Mortimo reason directly with Carole one-on-one. Convinced of his unique place within the movement, though, she was determined to focus on him and his circle of brethren. More than anything else, Carole wanted to learn to reason like him, and one day she summoned the courage to ask him directly to teach her. After a few moments reflection he replied: "Alright. But this Rasta business – when you're in it, you're in it!" Mortimo's statement alerts us to the fact that ethnographers do not simply choose their subjects but are just as often chosen by them.

Of this, Carole wrote, "His [Mortimo's] words were both cautionary and prophetic! As if to publicly acknowledge our arrangement, we then went to sit on the front porch facing the street and smoke the chalice together. And finally I engaged in reasoning as an active participant" (Yawney 1985a, 8).

Carole Yawney would proceed under the control, guidance and sufferance of Mortimo and it would be he, at least in the early years, who would determine the nature of reciprocities in their relationship. For his part, Mortimo had recruited an anthropologist for Rastafari – or at least for his position within the movement – who would work on behalf of his needs and goals. This was a move that would prefigure the kinds of subsequent ethnographer-subject collaborations (for example, Yawney's role as Planno's "recording secretary") that would be recognized within anthropology decades later. For her part, Carole had not only successfully aligned herself with *the* major centre of Rastafari activity in West Kingston, but with a cosmopolitan intellectual who had his own considerable history of travel and connections. These factors would significantly shape the description of the movement and its culture that Carole would produce over the years.

At Mortimo's "18 Fifth Street Open Yard and Rastafari Academy" in Trench Town, as she called it, Carole came to witness the comings and goings of the who's who of Rastafari: Bob Marley, Peter Tosh, Bunny Wailer, Roland Alfonso, Ras Michael, Bongo Herman, Jimmy Cliff, as well as elders like Ras Napier, Bongo Spence, Brother Wallace and Ras Trevor Campbell. She developed close relationships with those younger Rastafari who "came through Planno's hand"; these included individuals such as Harry T, Cudjoe Brown, Nabby Naturale and others whose names I have forgotten. Few, if any other outsiders, even in Jamaica, could claim the kind of access that Carole had negotiated. This was not just any yard – she had been installed at the Rastafari Vatican!

A covenant of kinds had been sealed between Goldilocks and the King of the Dreadlocks. Mortimo arranged for housing for Carole on Eighth Street in Trench Town and made everyone in his circle aware of her location as a means of providing for her security. West Kingston, it should be noted, was not a benign field site.[18] One had to know how to move here and one had to have protection. In this, she was under his charge – and many knew it. In exchange for his patronage and tutelage, she and her resources would be at his and his brethren's full disposal. With a white Volkswagen she had purchased, Carole would provide transportation and carry them around the island, facilitating their connections as necessary.

Figure 4.3 Carole Yawney and unidentified brethren, Eighth Street, Trench Town, 1970

This was an important, albeit underappreciated, feature of the spatial dimensions of her ethnographic practice. Her fieldwork was not simply a matter of co-residence with her subjects, but one of considerable movement, travel and visiting with them across the urban and rural landscape of Jamaica. The enhanced mobility that she provided to Mortimo enabled him to more readily mobilize brethren for meetings or "check for" brethren who resided at some distance. For Mortimo, she would be on call at all times of the day and night at a moment's notice. She could be, and was, dispatched at all hours of the night to retrieve one or more brethren for "personal reasonings" and political interventions that were critical to Mortimo's role as a Rastafari leader.

Carole's request of Mortimo to "teach her" had facets beyond learning how to reason and how to "move with Rastafari". Mortimo set her upon a reading campaign. She was assigned the *Philosophy and Opinions of Marcus Garvey* and Sylvia Pankhurst's *Black International* as key texts, and there was an incoming stream of pan-Africanist literature that she was expected to absorb. This included copies of the *Ethiopian Observer* and *African Opinion*, both journals that circulated through 18 Fifth Street, compliments of Brother Marks, an itinerant vendor of books and literature from Central Village, as well as materials from the Addis Ababa Bookstore on King Street run by Ras Lokai. Carole would become Mortimo's "study partner" – a term that he used – in various sessions of reasoning as well as his recording secretary. She played this latter role in typing notes from various meetings and preparing correspondence for him in his capacity as chairman of the Ethiopian World Federation Local 37. It should also be clear that Carole was enmeshed in a thoroughly reciprocal relationship with Mortimo. Based on her sensitivities to how Rastafari have responded to what has been written about them by scholars, Carole disseminated some thirteen copies of her dissertation to Mortimo and his circle after it was completed (see Yawney 1978). It was – as she noted to me – *the* read in Trench Town for the next several years! All of this followed from the injunction that "When you're in it, you're in it. Rasta a no turn-back thing!"

The statement by Bongo Poro at the head of this section is intended to suggest the significance that was attached to Carole's efforts in defining a "community" (or a specifiable social network of communicants) within which to do ethnographic research. Given the increasingly complex and heterodox nature of the movement from the late 1960s onward, both Carole and I have argued that locating oneself within a specifiable community or network of Rastafari is indispensable as a baseline for understanding something about the movement as a whole. This reflects the fact that the movement in Jamaica had already become more internally diverse and organizationally complex by this time and was beginning to develop "mansions" or houses with their own sectarian tendencies while being largely dispersed and decentralized around the island. This followed, in part, from developments after the visit of Emperor Haile Selassie I to Jamaica, and from political and demographic factors that dispersed members of the movement from areas of West Kingston like Back-o-Wall and Ackee Walk. By this time, certain earlier orientations or organizations – like the Howellites and the followers of Claudius Henry – had become marginalized within Rastafari and elements of their ideology had, as it were, "crystallized out" (Yawney 1972).[19]

In due course, Carole understood that she had aligned herself with a strongly pan-Africanist orientation within Rastafari – one that placed more emphasis on finding ways to "bridge the gap to Africa" than on the preoccupation with compliance with social codes such as "strictly Ital livity" (Yawney 1985b). Nowhere within the movement could Carole have been better positioned to describe and analyse its pan-Africanism or to witness and record the varied links that Rastafari maintained with Africa. In her writings she

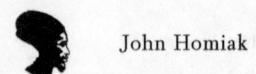
John Homiak

consistently emphasized and produced examples of the ways in which the Rastafari, from the inception of their movement, have been at the forefront of the movement to proclaim and promote an African identity for black people in the Caribbean and across the African diaspora (see Yawney 1999, 2004). For her, Rastafari needed to be seen as being at the centre of an epochal struggle over the definition of "who is African" (see Yawney 1999, 155–56).

"Grounding" as a Methodology of Initiation

> Within the portals of His Majesty, I-n-I have eyes of lightning within the reasoning. De I [is] suppose to know dat already – fi wi use dem to sort out the right people.
> – Bongo Wake-eye, 1996, Cypress Hall Nyahbinghi, Red Hills, St Andrew, Jamaica

In asking Mortimo to teach her, Carole was requesting, consciously or unconsciously, to become an active and engaged participant in the communal ritual of reasoning, a context defined as sacred by the Rastafari. At the time, the gendered space of reasoning represented the primary ritual activity of the Rastafari. This was the context in which the brethren prayed, in which elders demonstrated their charisma and coined ideology, in which new members were socialized, and through which all sought the inspiration of the divine. This is where participants came to explore each other's intellects, dispositions and varied abilities, and to know of another man "how 'im head stay". It was here that bonds of fellowship, community, respect and commitment were forged (see Yawney 1979; 1985; Homiak 1999). This is where individuals developed their own orientations of ideology and practice within the movement. For decades the Rastafari gathered all of these processes under a single omnibus term: grounding.[20]

Grounding constituted both Carole's methodology of initiation into Rastafari and ethnography as a form of human relationship. In choosing this path, Carole had opted for a particularly intimate way of being co-present with her subjects in "the field". She became an engaged participant in daily sessions of reasoning, taking communion with small face-to-face groups of brethren who shared the communion *chalice* (meaning the herbs pipe).[21] This involved her in hundreds (and ultimately thousands) of communal sessions in which ideology was being coined and the dynamics of an interpretive community were in play. She was, I would argue, the first researcher of Rastafari to take seriously the question of how we, as ethnographers of religion, could be co-present with the Rastafari in the context that they defined and experienced as sacred and inviolate. The fact that the dominant society both criminalized and trivialized Rastafari for the use of the *sacra* (herbs) made this all the more significant. Participation in reasoning meant being allowed into the intimate "backstage" of the culture at a time when Rastafari yards were still subject to raids by police.

Carole understood that this was a privilege that involved trust among participants. She also understood that there were trade-offs to such an experiential and initiatory approach. She did not get to dictate the flow of daily events or a schedule of research. Rather, she placed herself in the hands of Mortimo and his inner circle of brethren who would assume responsibility for her "training" (a term that they themselves used). Such a method was entirely non-directive and open-ended. If she was to be present as an active initiate in reasoning and co-present in the act of communion, there would be no note-taking and no tape recording. She would engage with the brethren on their own terms.

A challenge, however, remained. If Carole was to understand the relationship between the ingestion of the *materia sacra* and the reproduction of ideology within a sacred act of communion, how could she manage to recover the informational content of these sessions?[22] Because reasoning riffs the paradigmatic oppositions between the morally opposed domains of Zion and Babylon, it was easy enough to grasp such repeated semantic contrasts as those between black–white, high–low, in–out, over–under, or sight–blind that conformed to these two domains. But the expansive themes that might be covered in sessions of reasoning that might last for several hours would be harder to recall. To retrieve the content of these sessions, Yawney developed a method which she called "ganja mnemonics" that was her sole method of information capture during her probationary period. This was a kind of recall technique developed through a disciplined categorical memory practice. It is best to quote Yawney directly on this. She writes that her solution to retrieving the information flow of any given reasoning was

> to develop a set of symbols and signs of sufficient power to draw data from one state of consciousness into another, from the passive accepting state of the initiate into the lineal, critical state of the anthropologist. There were at least two kinds of data. One was of the informational sort – activities,

life histories, records of meetings and the like. The other consisted of more subjective data pertaining to states of mind, emotions and feelings, attitudes and values. It was less difficult to record the events of any one day than it was to reproduce a reasoning session of several hours duration . . . I used two methods. The first was to attempt to categorize the data as it was coming in. I used keywords which were intended to trigger off entire sections of conversation for me. As the subject changed I would add another signal to my list and mentally review it [the list] from time to time. All this would be happening [mentally] as I was also smoking herbs and participating in the sessions. At the first opportunity I would write the list down and try to elaborate upon it at my earliest convenience. Eventually, this data-coding process became an almost automatic procedure and I became free to absorb meaning on another level. By the time I became active in reasoning sessions, I could engage most of my attention units in the debate. In the writing of notes by this method I would meditate on a symbol and try to retrieve the state via this key. Then suddenly the scene would be recreated before my eyes like a movie and I could write it down. (Yawney 1985a, 13)

I can personally appreciate the effectiveness of this technique because during my own ethnographic fieldwork ten years later, I would independently invent the same technique in the course of my initial grounding with a cohort of Nyahbinghi elders. Based on our subsequent sharing of ideas and discussion of our convergent practices, I can say that what Carole produced was less than a verbatim transcript, but it was significantly more than simply a paraphrasing of ideas. In most cases the technique enabled us to reproduce extensive accounts of dialogue and discourse that included complete strings of statements that were exactly, or close to, verbatim. And with practice one becomes increasingly effective with the technique.

In Carole's case, it is important to point out that once she had become "seasoned" in reasoning and had increasingly gained the confidence of Mortimo and other brethren, he actually requested that she use her tape recorder in certain public and private meetings for his own record. In this way, she became his "recording secretary", accompanying him on his rounds to record his speeches in public, at church meetings and on ceremonial occasions.[23] At other times, when the perceived boundaries of the sacred where elevated during "backstage" moments, she would continue her use of ganja mnemonics.

In all of this Carole would continue to contend with the fact that she was a white woman within a strongly racialized and gendered space. It goes without

When Goldilocks Met the Dreadlocks

saying that Rastafari, while still patriarchal and racialized in varying degrees, has evolved considerably since the early 1970s. But at that time, patriarchal norms and Black Nationalist sentiments had a direct bearing on the nature of Carole's participation in Mortimo's circle. The fact that she was not only a woman but a white woman presented a challenge for both herself and Mortimo. Her sharing of the communal herbs pipe with the brethren represented a major anomaly within Rastafari culture because of the widely held Rastafari view of a woman's power to pollute with her menstrual issue.[24] In most quarters of the movement (for example, the House of Nyahbinghi) a woman's participation in reasonings would have been unthinkable and would never have been tolerated. Mortimo Planno was one of the few, perhaps the *only*, brethren who could have conditionally suspended the codes of patriarchy to enable such an incorporative manoeuvre for a white female researcher. In the vernacular of the period, he was "a different kind of Dread".[25]

Within his own group of brethren, however, this move elicited more than a little dissent and in some instances ambivalence toward Mortimo. In the early going, brethren who would "come on to the yard" would frequently "throw words" or "drop sounds" about "why mon [Mortimo] t'ink wi haffa sit een wid

Figure 4.4. Mortimo and Carole in Dungle, 1974

Figure 4.5. Hanging Ian Smith (prime minister of Rhodesia) in effigy, Trench Town, 1970 – Mortimo (bottom); Bob Marley (sans locks), Bunny Wailer and Peter tosh (standing centre), 1970

dis white ooman" (personal communication, Yawney). As a white woman, Carole was often singled out as a spy or identified as the "whore of Babylon", "Queen Eliza-bitch", the "White Witch of Rose Hall" and other epithets. More disturbing, there was frequent *susu*, or gossip, by some in Mortimo's circle (and many outside his immediate close network), that he was "dealing with" (having sexual relations with) Carole. She quickly became labelled by many as "Planno's white wife".[26] It is perhaps not surprising that Carole was consistently "fiya burned" by many in Mortimo's circle including Bob Marley, Peter Tosh and Bunny Wailer (personal communication, Yawney 1999).

In the face of these undercurrents, she had to competently perform her role by demonstrating and claiming her right to be present. Mortimo could be her guide initially, but she would have to deliver herself with resolve and "conscious sounds". This reflected the ethos among Rastafari that prevails to this day: that "every tub haffi siddong 'pon its own bottom". As a categorical representative of the white slave-master society, Carole would have to learn how to deliver herself with reasoning that was "tangible" [substantive] and "conscious" in Rastafari terms.[27]

I am certain that Carole would agree that the vicissitudes of the ethnographer were meaningful only for the insights they may have provided her into the ethos and spiritual worldview of the Rastafari. For it is in the process of rationalizing the holistic ideals of their worldview with the actual tenors of their lived experience that the Rastafari grappled with the existential contradictions faced by all religions and forms of spirituality (cf. Geertz 1973, 127–30). By this I mean that the *logos* of religious worldviews posit unity and harmony as one of their explicit qualities. We can understand this in terms of the desire of all religious or spiritual systems to "join in a common understanding of the cosmos [and to understand] how everything in the world is part of a *unified whole*" (my emphasis, Rappaport 1988, 16). As an African people, the Rastafari are keenly aware that their desire for oneness stands in stark contrast to the conditions of injustice and strife that characterize the historical circumstances of humanity at large and, more specifically, the conditions out of which Rastafari itself arose. Again it follows – and herewith the agonistics of the ethnographer – that unity and oneness can never be simple or sweet. Rather, the unity posited by the Rastafari can only arise out of an underlying tension and "argument" that is resolved in principle among specific participants, each of whom understand their own social and historic locations (white Europeans, Afro-Caribbeans).[28]

This suggests the key to appreciating Carole's work as an immersed and experimental ethnographer: the fact that *she could only truly grasp the meaning of Rastafari by becoming part of it.* She certainly became part of Mortimo's "fleshical" (biological) family.[29] Carole was one of the few academic outsiders to fully understand that to "move with" the Rastafari involved taking seriously their conviction that an ancient union between "knowing" and "being" was essential to being whole. Even today this remains the greatest challenge that Rastafari poses to researchers of the movement.[30] Transcending

John Homiak

Figure 4.6. Mortimo, Jeje and an unidentified sistren, 1970

the Cartesian dichotomy between self-and-other, knowing-and-being was simply one of the many ways in which Rastafari have validated their identity as "modern-antiques". For Carole, this oxymoron is embodied in one of the most simple of Rastafari truths: "Words without works is death." She became part of Rastafari through her "works" *for* Rastafari which would represent a lifelong commitment.

Becoming part of it, of course, did not happen for Carole all at once. It came about bit-by-bit through developing cultural competence and understandings (and later *overstandings*) that she began to develop through sessions of reasoning with Planno and his group. She has described how she came to master the creative and active use of the particular Rastafari lexicon used in reasoning (meaning, *I-ance* or *I-tesvar*; see Homiak 1995, 160–70), and, like the Rastafari themselves, to attend to phenomenon of synchronicity (or as outsiders might say, "coincidences") in "reading the signs of the times". Carole came to understand the respect that Rastafari had for "the holy herb" and its meanings as a symbol of comfort, inspiration and unity among the brethren over and against a hostile world. She became practised in "the proper use of herbs" (ganja) in terms of *suruing* or preparing the sacrament and the communion cup, blessing the chalice, as well as the manner of breathing appropriate to drawing from the chalice. In her own reflections on this initiatory path, she drew attention to the ways in which the Rastafari process of *grounding* facilitated an experience of inter-subjectivity and synchronicity. It was her experience that

> when several people share the impact of synchronicity, it creates a bond between them that is difficult to describe in words. A shared understanding brings the brethren closer together. Grounding is associated with smoking herbs together and during such occasions one often experiences inter-subjectivity. Sometime it is verbalized, but most often these shared understandings are acknowledged in nonverbal ways. Brethren regard this as a phenomenon of the heart center and thus no direct reference is required. (Yawney 1985a, 12)

The process of grounding, to be sure, has as its ultimate goal a radical transformation of consciousness that results in the decolonization of the mind. But, as is clear from Carole's experience, there were associated experiential and social aspects to this process that also involved the acquisition of a new complex of dispositions. Grounding was associated with a mindset that encouraged the individual to "move with the Irits" (Spirit) in an unpremeditated way and to free oneself from routines, agendas, schedules and "premeditation" – that is, to be in the present moment and open oneself up to any and all possibilities. For Carole, this came to mean keeping irregular hours and a willingness to travel to all parts of Kingston, day or night – movements that seemed to be spontaneously initiated by Planno and others in his circle. Bear in mind that this took some faith since West Kingston was not exactly a benign research environment. "Bleaching", or staying up all night with the chalice, also became a prerequisite for her. At one point during the early months of this process she reports sleeping only every other night. All this amounted to a form of incorporative ritual that made Carole part of Mortimo's inner circle and his wider social networks. Again, to make the point clear, Carole's quest for incorporation into the transcendental framework of the brethren was not the facile and sweet "One Love" of the reggae concert; it was the demanding discipline of a kind of "monastery".

From a social perspective, the thirty to thirty-five brethren who routinely visited Mortimo's yard became her "baptismal group" and the younger ones of this cohort shared with her the same "baptism of chalice". Her grounding, like that of the members of her baptismal group which was carried out over an extended period of time, produced a particular kind of social location within Rastafari that was attainable in no other way. Elsewhere, both Carole

John Homiak

and I have commented on the powerful bond that is created by this kind of grounding among brethren as roughly like-minded age-mates who "come up together in the faith". These peer groups, we argue, have traditionally constituted the elementary forms of the sociology of the movement inasmuch as these largely male age cohorts often coordinate over decades and share lifelong bonds of affiliation. It is through these social bonds – and their connection to one or more elders who provide tutelage to initiates – that an individual becomes identified and located within the wider polity.

In a movement that has always been highly decentralized and polycephalous, the experience of grounding can be mapped to specific camps and yards (or "scenes") within the cultural geography of Rastafari. Rastafari (and grounded ethnographers) carry these experiences with them as part of their ritual biographies and personal testimonies, often speaking with pride of having "passed through" places like "Egypt" (Back 'o Wall), "Shanti Town" (Foreshore Road), the Dungle, or Moonlight City.[31] Hence, from a researcher's point of view, a grounded ethnography is one that establishes a kind of pedigree of training in which the individual is known to have "come through the hand" of particular elders, moved through particular "scenery", and been associated with particular sets of age-mates or "grow-mates". These social aspects of grounding tend to become part of a Rastaman or Rastawoman's personal identity; they are carried with the individual as part of their personal testimony for the faith.

In relation to her later work on the globalization of Rastafari, Carole herself argued that her grounding – as both a kind of social location and pedigree – had a practical value because it was part of the reputation that would precede her everywhere she travelled in the Rastafari world.[32] In this regard, her grounding not only represented an essential aspect of her identity, but a form of cultural capital that she deployed to negotiate new relationships within the wider Rastafari polity. From a scholarly perspective, Carole's grounding – which represented both a body of knowledge and a high degree of performative cultural competence – provided her with a baseline for comparative assessment about differences and similarities between other forms of thought, expression and organization within Rastafari. This obtained in Jamaica as well as elsewhere.

In the early 1980s Carole routinely drew upon her grounding when she sought to connect with other Rastafari networks within the movement as part of a project to bring a delegation of Nyahbinghi Rastafari (led by Ras Boanerges) to Toronto. Her correspondence about this project with Klaus de

Albuquerque, a fellow ethnographer of Rastafari, is illustrative of the points made above:

> I myself knew very little about orthodox Nyahbinghi until I started work on the Voice of Thunder Project. When I was in Jamaica last June–July [1983] setting up the project, I spent every second day with Ras Boanerges [aka Bongo Watto/Henry Watson] and his brethren; the other days I spent with Mortimo and his circle – two mutually exclusive networks with some connecting links . . . I had a crash course in the Nyahbinghi stream of the movement which I hadn't had much contact with previously. It certainly helped to widen my perspective. Ras Boanerges is a real elder since he set up his base on Ninth Street in Trench Town in the late forties after having been associated with Howell at Pinnacle. His parents were Garveyites so he was well oriented to Pan-Africanism in his youth. He has a lot of stories to tell about Sam Brown, Planno, and Dizzy and others who grew in his yard. I worked in the early 1970s from Third Street up to Ninth Street [Trench Town] in Mortimo's network – yet never did he or any of them [his brethren] talk about Boanerges. Of course I didn't meet him. Without knowing his contributions to the movement that piece of the puzzle would never have fallen into place.[33]
>
> It has also helped me to understand Mortimo and his network's orientation much better. His circle is far more internationally/pan-African oriented than the more traditional Nyahbinghi brethren who, because of their social and cultural boundaries, emphasize *livity* or the purity of lifestyle much more. As well, they are more theocratic and Bible oriented than they are purely "political". (Letter to Klaus de Albuquerque, 19 February 1985, Papers of Carole D. Yawney, Correspondence Series, D-E, Smithsonian National Anthropological Archives)

This is one of many examples of how Carole became increasingly attuned to the multiple cultural and political orientations within Rastafari, or what I have elsewhere referred to as different "versions" of a highly dynamic culture (Homiak 1995, 130–31). As she became implicated in various initiatives to assist brethren to travel and represent Rastafari internationally (meaning international conferences and formal delegations of elders travelling abroad), Carole saw the contending figures/voices associated with these different orientations as central to the movement's politics of representation. She understood that the political impact of external factors on emergent Rastafari communities outside of Jamaica – their interplay with multiple orientations (for example, mansions) in Jamaica that could be represented abroad – represented a development that warranted greater scrutiny. She was clear that

John Homiak

Rastafari, as a large-scale, dynamic and heterogeneous movement, encapsulated multiple frames of reference that could at times be potentially contradictory (for example, black supremacy versus planetary humanism) and that certain themes – both by researchers and participants – might be variously "centred" or "de-centred", elevated or subordinated at any given period or point in time (Yawney 2002, 144–45). She understood as well that the discursive space that she occupied as an ethnographer with the Rastafari was not one of shared circumstances in which all were seen as having equal freedom and opportunity to speak or represent their particular orientation at any given point in time. Recognition of this diversity – this asserted "unity without uniformity" – was one of the reasons that Carole insisted that a researcher should generalize about the movement only with extreme caution.

The same contrasting orientations in ideology and social practice that she discerned between Mortimo's Ethiopian World Federation circles and the House of Nyahbinghi elders also led her to several important insights about the distinctive styles and capacities of participants in Rastafari as a community of speakers, all of which remains important to our understanding of the organizational and social dynamics of the movement. Here, I draw attention to the contrast Carole drew between "iterative" and "generative" as distinctive forms of discourse that are produced in the course of reasoning (Yawney 1985a). While the former is characteristically repetitive, formulaic and predictable and serves to recycle canonical truths, the latter is surprising, free-wheeling, and innovative and serves to authenticate the revelatory nature of the Rastafari quest for meaning and "overstanding".[34] Carole's ability to formulate this analytic distinction derived from her long-term and intensive participation in the activity of reasoning with speakers of quite varied intellectual, rhetorical and social abilities. In this regard she convincingly argued that these genres are tied to a similar contrast in different roles that may be adopted by Rastafari speakers – "preachers" versus "teachers" – respectively. Neither these roles nor their associated speech genres should be seen as mutually exclusive. Preachers, however, might be more comfortable with scriptural oratory and received truths whereas teachers might be more adept at fashioning provisional understandings that created new interpretations about the ways in which power was channelled between the domains of Zion and Babylon (see Yawney 1976). Carole's ability to discern these patterns and distinctions was the product of her rigorous "thick description" (Geertz 1973; Polier and Roseberry 1989, 247). Given their stature in the movement, it is perhaps worth nothing that Carole tended to see Ras

Boanerges and Mortimo – preacher and teacher – as archetypes of these respective roles and modes of discourse.[35]

Rastafari Outernational: Movements of Jah People

> We must become something for which our education and experience has ill-prepared us. We must become broader in scope, grander in vision, more courageous in outlook. We must become members of a new race, overcoming petty prejudice, owing our ultimate allegiance not to nation, but to our fellow men within the human community.
> – Emperor Haile Selassie I, Address to the United Nations, 3 October 1963

By the late 1980s Carole – based on her extensive travels in the Atlantic world – had come to realize that there were many more Rastafari outside Jamaica (and even outside the insular Caribbean) than in its "country of origin". By this time she had already become deeply involved in enabling Rastafari efforts to promote their own international outreach. She was, as I've noted above, the first scholar to write about Rastafari as a "travelling culture" (Clifford 1992; Yawney 1995). This included looking at how the traditional localizing strategies of cultural analysis have limited scholarly understanding of the movement's development as well as its more contemporary global spread. As I will outline below, her work in this regard involved the advocate and active organizing roles she played in assisting and participating in formal missions of travelling elders and a series of international conferences held in the Caribbean, North America and the United Kingdom (Yawney 1999, 177). Added to this was the run up to the movement's commemoration of the centenary of the birthday of Emperor Haile Selassie I of Ethiopia in 1992. This unfolded as an international event within the movement that served to revitalize Rastafari relations with the Ethiopian state, its people and the Rastafari settler community in Shashamane that had existed since the 1950s.

In developing a framework for the study of Rastafari globalization – at least one that went beyond merely tracing the overlapping routes of reggae music – Carole Yawney proved to be far ahead of everyone else in the field. A few points will suffice here. In her latter writings, Carole drew attention to the fact that increasing numbers of Rastafari from the diaspora had established footholds on the African continent in states other than Ethiopia. Others travelled to

John Homiak

and sojourned on the continent with frequency. This, she argued, constituted an important process of cultural exchange associated with Rastafari globalization that warranted attention against the background of the movement's traditional emphasis on repatriation (Yawney 1995, 59). Carole wrote about the symbolic ambiguity of iconic Rastafari symbols and the ways in which these symbols encouraged mediation between specific Rastafari concerns and practices and challenges faced by humanity at large, another factor relevant to the worldwide spread of Rastafari (Yawney 1992). And she was attentive to political and social forces within the global ecumene that tended to reinforce some long-held attitudes and practices within the culture or to support new innovations as part of the global spread of the movement. With regard to aspects of livity such as the Ital aesthetic, she noted that reciprocal exchanges between Jamaica and Rastafari communities abroad influenced by the health food movement served to promote innovation in Ital livity that enriched and developed it as a broader holistic health paradigm (Yawney 1985b). Carole also pointed to the ways in which Rastafari communities, under siege by the state abroad (for example, dealing with forms of discrimination and oppression through immigration policies or institutionalized racism), consciously embraced more "orthodox" forms of Rastafari livity for purposes of religious and cultural protection (Yawney 1995, 59–60). The combination of these factors, she argued, tended to encourage countervailing exchanges between the Jamaican Rastafari community and communities in North America and elsewhere as another feature of globalization. Finally, and related to this, Carole understood that the political and social contexts of globalization intensified the politics of representation within the movement in terms of what "version" of Rastafari was appropriate to travel and who was entitled to speak on its behalf. She understood that this has given rise to hegemonic formations within Rastafari itself that have gone largely unanalysed.[36]

In working to understand these processes, Carole's Trench Town grounding served as a resource that facilitated her access to, and connections within, Rastafari communities in the United Kingdom, North America and Ethiopia in addition to growing communities in the eastern Caribbean, Panama and Costa Rica, as well as South Africa. Writing nearly thirty years after her early fieldwork about the challenge of doing multi-sited fieldwork within various Rastafari communities in the Atlantic world and Ethiopia, she was clear about the many advantages that her intensive grounding had conferred upon her in researching the globalization of Rastafari from a comparative standpoint. She noted that, "like the Elders of Rastafari who travel on missions abroad, expe-

Figure 4.7b. Carole with Ras Ninni, Colón, Panama, 1999

Figure 4.7a. Carole with Bongo Rocky, Shashamane, 2002

rienced ethnographers can also step forward into the international Rastafari community with a sense of grounding. Having had an extended period of research in Jamaica, when I do visit other Rastafari communities in the diaspora I can plug into existing networks and accomplish a good deal in a short period of time" (Yawney 1999, 162).[37]

What Carole does not say in this context is that maintaining viability as an ethnographer doing multi-sited work involves an enormous personal and professional commitment in terms of continued networking, communication and sustaining relationships. I know of no other scholar who committed as much of her time to correspondence and networking as Yawney.[38] As a grounded ethnographer, Yawney would almost always make contact with someone in a community she was planning to visit, knowing that they would "check her out" through their own networks. This was, of course, precisely what she would have expected – and wanted.[39] She did this effectively in Trinidad, Barbados, St Kitts, the United States, the United Kingdom, Panama, South Africa and Namibia.

John Homiak

In the course of her travels, her grounding also positioned her effectively in relation to her participation in various international Rastafari conferences. In her writings, Carole went to some lengths to emphasize that while there is an explicit public dimension to much of the movement's globalization (for example, events such as Rastafari Focus held in London in 1986 or the Global Rastafari Reasoning at UWI in 2003), there is also far-ranging international networking activity that takes place in the "backstage" of these events that is typically not open to public scrutiny. In all of this she has emphasized the role that these conferences, and the networking they generate, play in relation to the development of Rastafari as a travelling culture and as a global phenomenon (Yawney 1999, 168–76). Her active involvement in many of these events brought her into contact (and sometimes conflict) with members of the emergent Rastafari intelligentsia that came of age in the late 1970s and early 1980s. This cohort included a mix of university educated and professionally trained Rastafari as well as younger "traditionalists", all of whom had their own grounding within the movement that included strategic ties with given elders. Carole drew attention to the activities of this intelligentsia for various reasons, one being the fact that they were a lightning rod for predictable tensions between a younger and older generation of Rastafari; another being that they gave rise to hegemonic formations within what has long been a counter-hegemonic cultural and political movement. In this latter regard, Carole was keenly attuned to the role that members of this intelligentsia played in shaping how Rastafari was publicly represented, particularly outside Jamaica. This awareness was shaped initially by Carole's involvement in the Toronto-based first Rastafari International Theocratic Assembly in 1982 and then by her attendance at the Caribbean Studies Association meeting held in St Kitts in 1983.[40] At the Rastafari Focus conference held at the Commonwealth Institute in 1986, Carole was, to my knowledge, the only white non-Rastafari scholar to present a paper. There, she discoursed on relationships between the state and the international Rastafari movement.

I believe it is useful here to outline a few of Carole's specific works within the international Rastafari arena. I have already mentioned that she began to collapse "the field" almost immediately after her initial fieldwork ended. In addition to facilitating a situation where her subjects came to her (as well as in the sense just outlined above), this idea of collapsing the field made sense with regard to the fact that there was a significant Rastafari community in Toronto, roughly half the population of that city being composed of immigrants. The field, as noted, was coming to her but not simply because of her ties with Mortimo. By the early 1980s (and with the global popularity of reggae music and Bob Marley), Rastafari had precipitated as a travelling culture (see Clifford 1992) with formal delegations of elders travelling to the eastern Caribbean and North America and with countervailing flows of Rastafari making what amounted to "pilgrimages" to Jamaica to connect with the roots of their culture. Part of this movement of people, symbols and ideas centred on the hosting of international Rastafari conferences, which themselves became increasingly important contexts for regional and global networking among Rastafari brethren and sistren from the early 1980s onward (see Yawney 1995). During this decade, Rastafari in Jamaica as well as across the Caribbean were increasingly challenged to defend their identity as Africans and their connections to the continent. It was during this period that the House of Nyahbinghi experienced something of a renaissance, a development that I have discussed elsewhere.[41] I believe it is fair to say that this development came about after the movement commemorated the Golden Jubilee anniversary of Emperor Haile Selassie I's coronation in November of 1980 with a month-long Nyahbinghi Assembly held in Jamaica and after the second International Rastafari Theocratic Assembly held in Jamaica in 1983. It was at this international gathering that the House of Nyahbinghi was named as the authoritative body on Rastafari teachings related to spiritual principles and the practice of livity.

Carole was in the middle of these developments as a co-organizer (with Masani Montague, a Jamaican-born Rastafari sistren) of the first International Rastafari Conference that took place at York University in Toronto in 1982. Ras Sam Brown, another legendary Rastafari elder, attended that gathering as its ranking figure. It was, to some extent, through her involvement with this first international conference that she began to engage with the issues of gender within Rastafari. She was, of course, intimately familiar with the ways in which women are marginalized within the discursive space of Rastafari – one dominated by male elders who serve as the organ of cultural knowledge. As a woman she was in sympathy with the position of the "Rastawoman" (see Sister Ilaloo 1981), maintaining close and supportive relationships with many Rastafari women. In the summer of 1983 both she and Sister Masani, a Toronto-based Rastafari woman, travelled to Jamaica independently to network with elders of the House of Nyahbinghi and lay the groundwork for the project. For her part, Sister Masani was consistently told by the brethren in Jamaica that she could not speak in any I-ssembly on this matter because she was a woman. At the time, this arose from the traditional Rastafari idea – which was defended by the

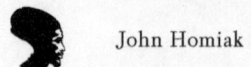

John Homiak

House – that "the man is the head" and that women should be "under the control of their kingman", and that they should not speak in the tabernacle. Sister Masani has referenced this experience in print and dismissed it as representing a lack of respect for the woman's point of view. She commented:

> In 1982 I went down to Jamaica to announce to the Nyahbinghi House the international conference I was organizing. When I got up to speak, three quarters of the crowd, who were men, ran out saying "Who is this woman? She has no right to speak in the House. She should go back to Canada and get the brothers to represent her . . . In Jamaica these are the restrictions that a Rastawoman must face. In the congregation she's not allowed to express her thoughts." (Littlejohn, Sheridan and Levine, n.d., 31)

Masani has not been alone in contesting the patriarchy of the movement. Sister Maureen Rowe (1980) had also become vocal on this subject at least two years previously, and there were also others.[42] I believe it was Carole's experience in Jamaica, coupled with her exposure to a rising tide of voices among the sistren internationally that made her come out in print on the subject of the dual oppression of women within Rastafari. She argued that being once oppressed by the dominant society as black women and twice oppressed by what amounted to "an explicit ideology of subordination", the status of women within Rastafari warranted a review within a movement which was about black liberation (see Yawney 1983a, 1983b, 1986). Mortimo Planno, in a sense, had prepared her for this. Among other things, what his cautionary words meant – "when you're in it, you're in it" – was that there could be no neutral stands within Rastafari! The struggle for liberation would appear everywhere and she would have to take responsibility for her own stand on whatever issues arose.

Carole has written that "The opportunity to move amongst Rastafari is a privilege that cannot be taken for granted but one that must be continuously re-evaluated and scrutinized according to the circumstances of each new situation" (1999, 154). She never felt that she could simply hide behind her identity as an anthropologist or ethnographer who was on the scene to simply record, analyse and report. Rather, within the context of a struggle for liberation, Carole felt that she needed to make a principled effort to enable and foreground Rastafari voices on a range of issues, from reparations and repatriation to gender relations, classism or colourism. This was clearly the case in terms of Carole's work on gender within the movement. But for her, as a privileged white academic, it was a stand that had to be nuanced in terms of a principle of Rastafari ethnography that she would repeatedly enunciate: "Never do anything to make an already oppressed and marginalized people more vulnerable." We see this principle elaborated in a response she wrote to a Jamaican sistren who had written asking her for information that might assist Rastafari sistren at large in their own liberation struggle within the movement. Carole outlined her position thusly:

> It has always been a challenge for me as someone from outside [Rastafari] to find ways to support Rastafari positively without closing my eyes to tensions within [the movement]. As a white woman, I have to move just so. I make a distinction between [Rastafari] family business and the public realm. Since Rastafari is so much under attack by the dominant culture and misrepresented in so many ways, I feel it my duty when writing or talking about Rastafari in public to try to set the record straight in a clear and no-illusions kind of way that will help. In other words, to inspire ones and ones to take Rastafari seriously as an African liberation energy – and to disabuse them of all racist stereotypes of Rastafari. From my perspective, [the fact] that African people are on the front line of genocidal attacks globally [means that] I cannot add any fuel to the fire of anti-African racism. (Letter to anonymous sistren, 1993, Papers of Carole D. Yawney, Correspondence Series, O-P, Smithsonian National Anthropological Archives)

With respect to the specifics of the gender struggle within Rastafari, she continued by saying that she has "witnessed much in Rastafari over the thirty-some years I have been involved. I know the situation of many sistren in Rastafari and their struggle. I have written about some of it in a way I hope will help. But I see my role as being in solidarity with sistren – giving support when asked. Within the backstage or family business context of Rastafari, I witness and then comment where it seems appropriate." Much could be said about Carole's work on gender in Rastafari, both in terms of her scholarly contributions and her practical support for Rastafari women seeking to redefine the woman's role in Rastafari, but suffice it to note here that she was the first non-Rastafari researcher to publish a perspective on the subordination of women within the movement (Yawney 1983a; 1983b; 1986; see also Sister Ilaloo 1981; Rowe 1985).[43]

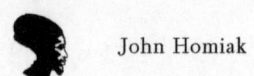

John Homiak

Rastafari and Anti-racist Activism: "Words without Works Is Death"

> I-n-I know that words without deeds is like a garden full of weeds. Words without works is death!
> – Earlites, Red Hills, St Andrew, 1999

As I noted above, knowing Rastafari for Carole meant becoming part of it. This meant finding ways that she, as a non-Rastafari, felt she could remain relevant to the goals and interests of the movement and work on behalf of Rastafari collectively; but it also meant finding ways that she could make certain Rastafari principles her own. Carole did this by using her institutional position to enable the travel and voices of key Rastafari brethren and sistren, by her extensive work with Rastafari in prisons, her expert court testimony on behalf of specific individuals and the principles of the Rastafari culture generally, and her wider anti-racist teaching and vocal activism that sought to educate others about the many ways in which African peoples were marginalized and made vulnerable by the dominant system.

In 1984 Carole Yawney, in collaboration with Sister Masani Montague, organized the first House of Nyabinghi mission to North America. Known as the "Voice of Thunder Trod", it was made by the patriarch Ras Boanerges and two younger brethren, Ras Iville Wright and Ras Iyenton McCoy. From this, she would go on to support Ras Boanerges's travel to "Rastafari Focus", an event convened under the auspices of the Rastafari Advisory Service (RAS) in 1986 held at the Commonwealth Institute in London. There, as the only white participant to my knowledge, she delivered a paper on relations between Rastafari, the legal system and the state that reflected on her own advocacy work with/for the movement and which reflected on the repeated pattern of oppressive reactions by the state to Rastafari, be it Jamaica, England, Canada or the United States.

Much of her work during the 1980s was used to tie together the foundations of a multi-sited ethnography that revealed the ways in which Rastafari events and initiatives were creating linkages and resonances across various locations of the black Atlantic and creating what could truly be called an international community. Among these influences was the impact of an internationally distributed newspaper called *Rastafari Speaks* that began to be published in Trinidad by Shango Baku and Sekou Tafari in 1980. Despite a pattern of confiscation by police there, it was this ephemeral publication,

Figure 4.8. Carole Yawney addressing the audience at "Rastafari Focus", Commonwealth Institute, London, 1988 (Ras Historian, far left, behind)

Carole has argued, that not only mobilized Rastafari in the eastern Caribbean, but promoted international participation in the first and second international conferences in Toronto, Canada (1982), and Kingston, Jamaica (1983) (Yawney 1995, 65–66).

From the early 1970s, Carole developed an understandable interest in the representational politics surrounding the movement, that is, the ways in which the scholarly and popular published works as well as the media – via reportage, films or popular portrayals – shaped or distorted information about the movement and its members. Sensitivity to who spoke for the movement and how it was represented, given its "versions" and contending voices, is also something that Yawney wove into her ethnographic work and advocacy on behalf of Rastafari. During the 1990s until her passing, she began to turn her attention to communities on the African continent, firstly in

John Homiak

South Africa which she began visiting in the mid-1990s, and where a nascent Rastafari movement influenced by reggae had emerged in the late 1970s and had shaped part of the anti-apartheid struggle. In her South African sojourns – variously to Cape Town, Paarl, Johannesburg, Knysna and Kimberly – Carole served as Planno's international patron by faithfully linking him in Jamaica via Bush Radio (the oldest radio station in the Cape) with Rastafari radio hosts such as Ras Elphy and Ras Pakai in South Africa. This was a strategic move on Carole's part and reflected how she worked to shape the movement's politics of representation on the continent. Because the media frequently has portrayed Rastafari as "fanatics" devoted to Emperor Haile Selassie and fixated on Ethiopia, this obscured their more general pan-Africanism and concern with African liberation movements. In one of her Bush Radio linkages with Mortimo, he delivered a message about Bob Marley and African unity without once bringing Ethiopia into the picture:

> Now there is a Bob Marley who was a rude boy which is a different Bob Marley from the Bob Marley that I-n-I know. Yes I! So, we're going to mould Bob Marley from [. . .] Bob Marley the rude boy into [. . .] Bob Marley the Rasta messenJAH who carry Jah message throughout the whole world. So that was the purpose of having Bob Marley in Trenchtown, that we use Bob Marley as our messenJah who carry the messages around the whole world that today I can able feh be talking to my brethren and sistren in South Africa about Bob Marley today being his birthday. Good! *So we want Africa to know from our perspective the purpose of using Bob Marley as a messenger who have done us great to link with Africa with us in the Caribbean and in the West Indies and throughout the whole Western Diaspora with Africa.* (Mortimo Planno 1997; quoted and emphasis added in Yawney 1999, 157)

In 1999, while Mortimo was still the first resident scholar at the newly formed Folk Filosofi Unit at the University of the West Indies, Carole and I, along with her colleague and pan-Africanist educator Menkowra "Clem" Marshall, videotaped our interview with him, which could be shared with multiple Rastafari communities in South Africa during an upcoming trip that she was taking.

This tape was augmented with a performance of Nyahbinghi chanting and oral testimony by several Nyahbinghi elders, including Bongo Shephan and Bongo Tawney. In the year 2000 when I was in Cape Town with Carole, she again made the Bush Radio link with Mortimo, this time involving both of us as speakers on Bush Radio with the Jamaican-born Nyahbinghi matri-

When Goldilocks Met the Dreadlocks

Figure 4.9. Mortimo in a videotaped interview with Menkowra "Clem" Marshall and John Homiak, Taylor Hall, University of the West Indies, Mona, 1999

arch, Mamma Beryl, who had repatriated herself to South Africa while on a mission there with Bongo Time in 1996.

This was entirely typical of Carole. Both in her movements within and between Rastafari communities and in her contacts with progressive scholars, she would link progressive forces, both Rastafari and non-Rastafari. In addition to the role that Yawney came to play as a "connector" and broker for Rastafari, the particular South African sojourn also highlighted another of the roles that Yawney developed for herself as an itinerant Rastafari ethnographer – one which we both shared. This was her and my role in collecting and putting into circulation Rastafari materials acquired on various field trips (for example, broadsides, photographs, newsletters, pamphlets, Rasta artwork and videos). This was one of the ways in which she/we collapsed various parts of the international community for our Rastafari hosts – be they in Panama, Johannesburg, Trinidad, Shashamane, or Washington, DC.

On the trip that we made to South Africa in 2000, Carole and I purchased thirteen copies of the *Holy Piby* (published by Rastafari publisher Miguel Lorne of Headstart Books) and, in connection with Moses Mugwiti, an African journalist, we ritually "repatriated" this publication to Africa through a story in the *Cape Times* (see "*Holy Piby* Brought Back to Africa: The Return of the Black Man's Bible", 29 May 2000).[44] We then gave the copies of the *Piby* to members of the Marcus Garvey camp in Philippi, the Burning Speak Camp in Parkwood and to various other Rastafari who were part of Yawney's network.

In 1997 Carole formally launched a joint effort on our part called the International Rastafari Archives Project. She did this by depositing copies of Rastafari materials at the University of the Western Cape. The idea was initiated by her; but it came about because we both came to realize that between us – two

John Homiak

researchers with over fifty years of combined experience with Rastafari – we had acquired an impressive body of ephemeral Rastafari materials. In some instances, this involved holding full runs of ephemeral series that the Rastafari publishers of these materials no longer had themselves.[45] Carole recognized that collaboration with Rastafari by sharing this data and feeding it back into communities could potentially greatly facilitate our understanding of the movement. She also recognized that this kind of sharing was timely given the fact that the globalization of the movement coincided with the coming of age of a generation of scholars, organizers and activists who were themselves Rastafari (a Rasta intelligentsia, if you will), who all had an international presence and played a key role in developments within the movement. Carole's and my perspective was/is that their input provides a necessary and desired challenge to the intellectual hegemony of non-Rastafari researchers like ourselves, if only because this foregrounds issues about our own ethical responsibilities and the limits of our representational authority (see Yawney 1999, 164–65).

For Carole, all of this was an extension of the scrupulously ethical manner in which she went about making her own representations of Rastafari within the scholarly world. Carole had a practice of ensuring that at least a few Rastafari were present when she delivered papers about the movement and their culture, and she actively solicited feedback from them. This began in her Trench Town days when she circulated at least a dozen copies of her four-hundred-page dissertation among Mortimo and his circle. She wanted them to know and understand what she was saying about them. And it carried over into the most professional of arenas. When she delivered a paper on Rastafari globalization at the 1995 meetings of the American Anthropological Association in Washington, DC (along with myself, Barry Chevannes and Werner Zips), five Rastafari were present, including two Trinidadian-born Rastas who travelled with her from Toronto, Canada. I witnessed the same thing when we presented a joint paper at the Caribbean Studies Association in Panama City, Panama, in 1999 and in Pretoria, South Africa, in 2000. Prior to our session in Panama at the Caribbean Studies Association, we made contact with several Rastafari in Panama City and Colón, and she insisted that they attend the session. In South Africa our movements were exclusively with Rastafari representing three separate communities and ultimately Carole travelled to Pretoria with three Rastafari, one of whom, a Rastafari matriarch who had repatriated from Jamaica, delivered the paper I had prepared.

Space does not allow me to elaborate on all of the ways in which Carole Yawney served as an activist and advocate for Rastafari. I will close by briefly noting three other areas in which she made significant commitments: her work with Rastafari prisoners, expert testimony within the legal system and her work with MOVE[46] and the case of Mumia Abul Jamal. Beginning in the early 1980s, Yawney started to become deeply involved in prison work in places that included Attica and Greenwood in upstate New York. One of the prisoners with whom she worked in Attica was named Jah B, a Rastafari who credited Planno as his mentor.

With respect to legal representation, Carole began working in this area for Rastafari even before her dissertation was finished. Her groundings with Planno meant that she took seriously Rastafari claims for their use of cannabis as their sacrament as well as for their right to hold an Ital diet for both spiritual and holistic health reasons.[47] She brought her understandings of this to bear both in court and in relation to the religious programmes and chaplaincy services that were either extended to or withheld from Rastafari who were incarcerated, and spent considerable energy in dealing with prison administrators and chaplains on these matters. And perhaps most importantly, Yawney made regular visits first to Attica and then to Greenwood (upper New York State) to visit Jah B and other incarcerated Rastafari, and also corresponded with these individuals.

In the area of expert testimony it should be pointed out that Yawney served as an expert witness in no less that twenty-eight court cases involving Rastafari. This included two very high profile constitutional challenges in court: that of Jamaican Rastafari Dennis Forsythe in his constitutional challenge before the Supreme Court of Jamaica on Rastafari religious freedom (regarding the sacramental use of ganja) and that of Ras Garreth Prince in the Constitutional Court of the Republic of South Africa, Western Cape, on a similar matter. Prince was lawyer and had passed the bar but was banned from practising law because of his acknowledged use of cannabis. Both of these were major cases in which Yawney was apparently the only scholar willing to step forward.

Finally, there is the case of MOVE and Mumia Abul Jamal with which she first became involved in 1995. Mumia Abul Jamal, a former journalist and a former Black Panther who wears locks, has been in prison since 1981 for the accused murder of a Philadelphia policeman. Around the world he is widely considered to be a political prisoner because of his outspoken criticism of the American criminal justice system in relation to blacks and the many irregularities with his trial and conviction. MOVE is a Philadelphia-based group of blacks who wear their hair in dreadlocks and have been criminalized by

John Homiak

Figure 4.10. MOVE gathering, York University, Toronto, 1995. Left to right: Ras Iville Wright, Ras Iration I, Rev. Ishakamusa Barashango and Rubin "Hurricane" Carter (far right); Carole (kneeling, bottom left).

the media for confrontations with police that dated back to the late 1970s. In 1995, shortly after a major Rastafari conference in Toronto (which included Ras Boanerges, Ras Sam Brown, Bongo Time, Ma-Ashanti and Ras Iration I from Jamaica), Carole engaged various members of the Toronto Rastafari community in a cross-campus programme at York University held in solidarity with Mumia and MOVE. The programme included an address by Ras Iration I, another Jamaican brethren with whom she worked, in outlining the similarities in the struggle shared by MOVE, and the Rastafari and black people in Philadelphia and Toronto, respectively.

The following year when Yawney visited Jamaica, she held an extensive study session with Planno and a number of his brethren that involved educating them about MOVE. And as the internationalist that she was, she would ultimately carry the MOVE cause to South Africa with Planno's endorsement and ground it there as well. Space does not allow an ample discussion of all of Yawney's work with MOVE, but suffice it to note here that this is just one example of the way in which the long-term relationship she had with Planno as student–teacher was reciprocal. As she came to serve as his eyes and ears aboard, she was sometimes the teacher and he the student.

Conclusion

> The opportunity to move amongst Rastafari is a privilege that cannot be taken for granted but one that must be continuously re-evaluated and scrutinized according to the circumstances of each new situation.
> – Yawney 1999, 154

As the first truly long-term participatory ethnographer of Rastafari and the first white female ethnographer, Carole Diane Yawney was a pioneer in Rastafari studies. Because of her own intensive grounding by one of the movement's most historic figures and her own activist and participatory approach, she was someone who routinely confounded the "insider–outsider" dichotomy for Rastafari. In any given context, she would invariably find herself navigating both insider and outsider positions. A consummate diplomat, "skillful means" was a phrase that she lived by in this work. If it can be said that many indigenous communities in the twenty-first century have come to have their "own" ethnographers – this due to a new emphasis on collaboration, trust and transparency – then Carole Yawney was indeed *the* ethnographer not simply *of*, but *for* the Rastafari. In all of her work as both an academic and an activist, she went to great lengths to carefully position her voice with respect to the culture and the community – and to be seen neither as "speaking about" nor "speaking for" Rastafari, but as "speaking with" brethren and sistren. All of this reflected the fundamental respect she had for her subjects, many of whom – like Mortimo Planno – she engaged as active and mutual collaborators, and who treated her similarly.

With respect to her published ethnography, despite having never produced a monograph-length account of Rastafari, she has given us what is arguably the richest "thick description" of the movement's culture and religious life. Her attention to the social construction of space and the mutable boundaries around the sacred (Yawney 1979; 1985a), her insights regarding Rastafari attitudes and constructions of race and nationality (Yawney 1976) are all the product of a deep immersion and participation within the culture. Her understanding of "visionary experience", as seen through the portals of Rastafari as a community of speakers who produce distinctively different registers of speech that are aligned with and flow from the creativity of the varied rhetorical and intellectual abilities of given speakers, is among her most insightful contributions to the literature (see 1985a).

John Homiak

Nearly everything she has researched and written about regarding the globalizing processes and challenges related to Rastafari will serve as paths to be followed and enriched by a new generation of researchers of the movement – both Rastafari and non-Rastafari. Her analysis of Rastafari as a "travelling culture" alerts us to the spatial challenges that Rastafari poses to researchers and the need for innovative multi-centred forms of research in the global sphere. With regard to how we, collectively as researchers from different disciplinary backgrounds using different methods, actually come to "know" Rastafari, Carole was clear that there are no unmediated social facts that can provide direct access to the movement's operative discourses. I know that she would continue to argue that the field remains overdue for a sociology of knowledge approach to assessing the ways in which scholars and participants construct knowledge about the culture. This would hardly surprise the Rastafari themselves who, for decades, have insisted they are here to "confound the wise and prudent".

In the sphere of Rastafari globalization, Yawney's grounded approach put her years ahead of everyone else. But we should be clear that this reflected a phenomenal commitment, personally and professionally. Carole directed her prodigious energies to sustaining personal relations on at least four continents and she devoted much of her personal finances to Rastafari "works" which included assisting Rastafari and pan-African colleagues to travel internationally. She made optimal and strategic use of her grounded ability to "move with" Rastafari in a broad range of transnational situations and she enlisted colleagues like myself, as well as members of the Rastafari intelligentsia, in the overall effort. To date, Carole has posed many of the major queries related to the challenges that globalization poses for Rastafari. Identifying a tension between the proclaimed status as a universal faith for all and as a black heritage to be guarded by some, she questions whether the movement will fully overcome its Caribbean-centric focus. And noting the growing foothold that Rastafari communities have on the continent, she has asked how the movement's Ethiopianist and pan-African sensibilities will ultimately be harmonized. These and other questions will no doubt continue to engage researchers of the movement now and in the future. But whatever research agenda Carole might have been pursuing, she was continuously seeking to make her writing and her "works" relevant and meaningful to the Rastafari themselves. She took seriously the Rastafari warning that "words without works is death" and she routinely drew brethren and sistren into her projects as active and equal consultants. This was most abundantly clear in the path that we followed in launching a proposal for what would become the "Discovering Rastafari!" exhibition at the Smithsonian. It was upon Carole's insistence that we first present this proposal to the Rastafari community in Shashamane, Ethiopia – the land that the brethren and sistren know as home.

With all of this, I believe – or rather *I know* – that Carole Yawney's contribution to the movement transcended her writings and the documentary record she leaves behind. Her greatest contribution rests with the profound and continuing impact that her presence had within the movement, her presence as a representative of her race and nationality – as a white, Ukrainian-Canadian woman. Carole never professed a Rastafari identity. In fact she frequently declared herself publicly as an "outsider" to Rastafari. But she was an outsider who, in her own eclectic spirituality, took Rastafari spirituality very seriously. I know that she accepted the Rastafari maxim that "no one is truly free unless everyone is free" and that this could never happen until Africa and all African people were totally liberated. Carole manifested these anti-racist principles in her writings and in her works. Perhaps most importantly, she modelled back to her Rastafari brethren and sistren the very principles of His Imperial Majesty that they had presented to her. One of her collaborators, Ras Iyenton, who had been on the mission with Ras Boanerges to Toronto in 1984, reflected on her works in a conversation:

Figure 4.11 Mortiom Planno in the Dungle, circa 1970

> Wi never see no one like her before. Carole was the first person to come and live in West Kingston – yeah, really live dere – with the Rasta and the badman dem. Serious 'ing, ya know. She was really very, very brave. And she continued her works from them time. I know His Majesty must have been her guide – is the only way she coulda guh through. Even more than a lot of Rastafari people dem, His Majesty was her guide. Sister Carole lived up – mi say lived up! – to I-n-I livitical expectations – *fully*!

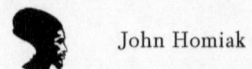 John Homiak

Postscript

Carole Diane Yawney became a "member of a new race" long before her cosmic transition on 23 July 2005 – earthstrong 113 of His Imperial Majesty. This transformation took place because she had become part of a community of liberators – not the least of whom was Ras Mortimo Planno. From the time of their initial covenant, Mortimo assigned them special names. She would be *Sampaku*; he would be *Raspaku*. Both worked according to the movement's radical pedagogy of the Irits (Spirit) that "each-one-teach-one". Raspaku himself surely grew and changed because of his lifelong relationship with Sampaku. That story remains "the half not yet told". On the day of Sampaku's transition, Raspaku – due to the onset of gangrene – had to have his right leg amputated. Of them, Professor Barry Chevannes would later say: "If ever two souls were one, these were they."

Acknowledgements

All photographs in this chapter are taken from the papers of Dr Carole D. Yawney. Courtesy of the National Anthropological Archives, Smithsonian Institution.

Notes

1. I have used the couplet "Goldilocks/Dreadlocks" to highlight the obvious way in which "race" relations were evoked by Carole Yawney's fieldwork and the mutual collaboration between her and Mortimo Planno, but also to underscore the fact that both parties managed to bridge profound differences in class, culture and nationality in evolving an anti-racist stance that modelled the teaching of Emperor Haile Selassie I on anti-racism.
2. The papers of Carole D. Yawney and the International Rastafari Archives Project, which she and I began, are now housed in the Smithsonian's National Anthropological Archives at the Smithsonian Museum Support Center, Suitland, Maryland. The National Anthropological Archives are part of the broader anthropological programme directed by the author.
3. The relationship was wholly reciprocal but as the junior partner I always felt

that because of Carole's experience and insights I benefited disproportionately from our collaboration.

4. During the 1970s Yawney recorded quite a number of public presentations and reasonings by Planno. Presently, there are some twenty-five or more audiotapes of him and his associates from this period in the Smithsonian's National Anthropological Archives. Recordings of events and reasonings were also made in 1969 by Professor Lambros Comitas during the ganja study in Jamaica, funded by the National Institute of Health. This runs counter to Rupert Lewis's assessment that even though Planno and a few others were to Jamaica what Malcolm X was to the United States, "... the work done by Planno got no media coverage and there is no record of the speeches and talks given or the reasonings that took place" (Lewis 1998, 101–2).

5. The 1970s is a period of Rastafari studies that warrants more attention in terms of the contrasting methods and research interests of Owens, Chevannes, Yawney, Nettleford and, later, Klaus de Albuquerque, among others. Suffice it to note here that Owens worked with a broad range of informants across West Kingston and rural Clarendon. By all accounts, his work was highly participatory but his interest in systematizing and presenting a coherent Rastafari theology tends to obscure any sense of the sociology and material relations of the movement. Chevannes's initial work tended to focus on many of the first preachers of the movement, particularly the group of Robert Hinds, and later navigated through the dreadlocks orientation. While Chevannes, Owens and Yawney were all present among Rastafari at the sufferance of the brethren, Yawney – through her living arrangements on Eighth Street in Trench Town – was arguably the only one of the three to place herself fully under their tutelage and control. Like others, she had research interests that she pursued; but unlike others, she became a member of a specific community of Rastafari.

6. Until about the mid-1990s, when Rastafari became more prominent on the Internet, the parameters of "cultural intimacy" among the Rastafari functioned to silence the discussion of certain topics in the presence of outsiders. This would have included such things as the existence of colour and, to a lesser extent, gender discrimination among Rastafari themselves. These norms of cultural intimacy not only serve a community defining function, they stand as a challenge to the understandings and knowledge that ethnographers seek to produce. On cultural intimacy, see Herzfeld (1997).

7. In gauging the mood of the country toward Rastafari at the outset of the 1970s, Errol Bowen (1971, 41) cited the negative views of *Gleaner* colum-

nist Clinton Parchment who wrote, "it is self-evident that the majority [of Rastafari] are lazy, dirty, violent and lawless scoundrels mouthing religious phrases to cover up their aversion to work and their ill habits".

8. Simpson's publications on Rastafari were attacked in the *Gleaner*. The movement, its members and their beliefs were, in effect, seen as unworthy of academic study. The article labelled the beliefs of the "cultists" as blasphemous and Simpson's work as a scandalous and misguided waste of intellectual effort.

9. A liminar is an individual in a liminal or "betwixt and between" status. By their own definition of themselves as Africans in exile, Rastafari are liminars. They are in transition from physical captivity in Babylon to repatriation and redemption in Zion.

10. Part of Planno's New York connections derived from the fact that in 1963 he sent Ronald Pennycooke and Ras Dago [Whitney Turn] to New York to launch their own unofficial mission to Ethiopia in the aftermath of the unofficial mission by Filmore Alvaranga, Douglas Mack and Samuel Clayton during that same year. Pennycooke and Dago never travelled beyond New York (personal communication, Brother Gabriel Diaz 2006).

11. For a movement that originated in the Caribbean, these connections are hardly surprising given that all manner of global flows and connections have historically been routed through the region. It remains the case, however, that with a few exceptions, these kinds of links remain under-theorized by scholars in assessing the formation and development of the Rastafari movement (see Gilroy 1993, 17; 227; Hill 1981; Carnegie 1999; Yawney 2002).

12. In cultural anthropology this contrast between "the field" and "home" represents a time-honoured dichotomy found in the natural sciences, whereby the collecting of data is done "there" (in the field) and the interpreting, analysing and writing up of one's findings is done "here" (at home; at the university). This dichotomy has often been used to construct a false sense of objectivity for different kinds of work in the social sciences. It is now generally accepted that all perspectives on social phenomena are necessarily mediated from some specific perspective.

13. It can be argued that, from its inception, Rastafari has been postmodern in terms of its ability to disrupt and contest master narratives, defy categorization, and travel across boundaries of race, class, language, ethnicity and nationality. For her part, however, Carole abhorred academic fashion, especially the proliferation of postmodern jargonism that she felt obscured the realities of oppression and struggle in the lives of real people.

14. The conference to which Yawney alludes was the annual meetings of the Caribbean Psychiatric and American Psychiatric Associations held in Ocho Rios in May 1969. The paper referred to was given by Dr Raymond Prince. During the conference, a group of Rastafari led by Mortimo Planno were allowed to participate in a panel discussion led by Dr Vera Rubin, director of the Research Institute for the Study of Man (RISM) and Dr Ari Kiev, a well-known transcultural psychiatrist.
15. Planno repeatedly told Carole, lest she become too complacent, that she should "Never make the mistake of assuming you have friends within Rastafari." In 2005, while attending the first Rastafari Hispanic summit in Panama City with various Jamaican-born Rastafari, I was publicly reminded of my own indeterminate probationary status by a Nyahbinghi elder with whom I had congenial relations. He said, "Jake, all of [the] works I-n-I have seen you do over the years is all positive – but just remember, the scrutiny don't stop."
16. Literally, of "weak heart", but from a Rasta perspective, someone who is timid or fearful and therefore not fully whole. Such individuals are deemed unworthy to stand within the portals of Rastafari. The term acquires significance within the culture inasmuch as Rastafari consider their identity and movement as one of "the heart".
17. I believe it is fair to say that Planno and those in his inner circle used these tests and ordeals to strategically assess Yawney's merits, and to determine the pace at which she should either be "brought in" to or continue to be "screened off" from knowledge of his works and activities. It is difficult to know precisely when acceptance was gained with specific individuals, but it is clear that within her early years Carole became a member of Mortimo's "fleshly" and spiritual family.
18. Carole was kidnapped at knifepoint during the first year of her sojourn in Trench Town by a disturbed individual from the area. The drama played out across the urban landscape and she was eventually rescued by the infamous policeman Joe Williams.
19. During her initial fieldwork, Yawney, Chevannes and Owens did collaborate on one field trip to Greenbottom, Clarendon, where they met with Claudius Henry and his congregation. This followed up on work in which Barry Chevannes was previously engaged (see Chevannes 1976).
20. Yawney and I, through many discussions between us as well as reasonings with elders, feel that "grounding" held sway as a more or less coherent set of practices from roughly the early 1950s through the late 1980s. We

believe that grounding – especially through its association with reasoning and the sharing of the communal herbs pipe – was the primary means by which individuals became Rastafari during these decades in Jamaica. I would argue that shifts in the demographics of the movement, the emergence of Rastafari as a travelling culture, and various media-driven aspects of Rastafari popular culture have altered the importance of grounding within the culture.

21. For my part, I view the lack of critical commentary on this topic to be something of a blind spot in the literature on the movement. It is certainly the case that any researcher doing actual ethnographic work on Rastafari from the 1970s onward would be confronted by the connection between herb use and Rastafari sociability as a boundary defining issue. Abstinence would entail a very different or limited familiarity with the brethren in most cases. Whatever the actual practice might have been for other specific individuals (for example, Nettleford, Owens, Chevannes), Carole was the only researcher to address this openly as part of her ethnographic practice. It is telling, I believe, the extent to which much of the contemporary literature on Rastafari (see, for example, Murrell, Spencer and McFarlane 1998) wilfully ignores the role of cannabis in the culture as the basis for sociability and communion, *material sacra,* substance of symbolic exchange, or as an economic commodity.

22. Yawney actually continued this approach throughout her career. She rarely asked direct questions of brethren or sistren but continued to "move with the Spirit" among Rastafari with the expectation that, as she would frequently say, "If you open yourself to the Universe, the world will come in."

23. According to her own account, Planno began to refer to her as his "secretary" and requested that she type many of the letters of correspondence that he wrote as the head of the Ethiopian World Federation Local 37. Her typing for him included letters to the editor of the *Gleaner*, broadsides, copies of plays and poetry and the correspondence he had on a delicate political matter with the settler community in Shashamane, Ethiopia (Yawney 1985a, 14).

24. In retrospect, I must confess that Carole and I never discussed how Planno and his circle dealt with Yawney's menstruation, meaning whether she voluntarily withdrew from ritual activity or whether the whole issue was somehow ignored.

25. During the 1970s and 1980s, this phrase was frequently used by Rastafari to signal the level of individualism that existed within the movement with

each brethren being accorded the freedom, within certain limits, to establish their own orientation in the culture. Planno clearly had an ability to stretch those limits.

26. The drama to which their collaboration gave rise certainly reflected the fraught nature of race relations among the brethren, but the label never fit the reality. Mortimo was a determined racial separatist when it came to the black man as a progenitor and head of the family. And he was well-known for his articulation of "the buffer [brown] pickney syndrome" (see "Earth's Most Strangest Man"), a critique he fashioned of the role that racial amalgamation played in the class–colour system of post-plantation Jamaica. For Carole, this separation of the races was all part of the conscientizing that she acquired through Mortimo and a Rastafari principle that she came to understand.

27. The Rastafari–researcher interface is something that rarely gets sufficient elaboration, even in scholarly work. Father Joseph Owens, who worked in West Kingston during the same time that Carole did, wrote that "reasoning is not for milquetoasts", and left it at that. As with Carole's work, this must be seen as a form of self-censorship that underplayed the ordeals to which she was subjected out of respect for the history of marginalization and oppression that black people and Rastafari have endured. Much the same can be said of Barry Chevannes. It is only through a close reading of Chevannes' book and his work with the Nyahbinghi House that one comes to recognize the scrutiny and tests to which he too was subjected (see 1994, 209–12). One hopes that with the maturation of Rastafari studies and the movement itself, these realities will be more fully recognized.

28. The Rastafari term "argument" is notable here primarily because it does not map the same semantic referents or connotations as its standard English equivalent. "Argument" refers to a set of propositions or claims about social and historical reality that are subject to collective scrutiny, analysis and debate. It has little to do with an incendiary speech act between two individuals but rather suggests the expression of propositions that may have their own validity but call out for incorporation into a larger holistic understanding or *overstanding*. An "argument" in this Rastafari sense is thus a starting point for dialogue. What Carole came to "overstand" or "I-verstand" within Rastafari is that while some arguments may be "ignorant", "void", or "vain" – and were to be dismissed as such – the process of argument, as in reasoning, was linked directly to the transcendent value that Rastafari place on a collective quest for oneness. As central to Rastafari praxis, this search

for oneness – this realization of holism within the "I" – can never be fixed or static but must embody a *notion of a unity that exists only through tension*.

29. Carole was an intimate member of Mortimo's biological family and was close to his wife JeJe (or otherwise Joycie) and knew his biological children. When Jeje passed away in the mid-1980s, Carole was in Jamaica within twenty-four hours and functioned to broker the funeral arrangements and memorial.

30. We are dealing here with the logos of "I" and the Rastafari concept of the "modern-antique". It is noteworthy that other scholars of the anthropology of religion focus on the same feature of knowing-and-being as part of an existential holism for all religious systems of thought (Rappaport 1988, 16; Fernandez 1986) and have similarly noted that the essential function of all ritual metaphors is to signify a "return to the whole".

31. The Rastafari phrase of having "passed through" is less frequently heard among Rastafari today for understandable reasons. This phrase does not simply reference a familiarity with, or affiliation to, particular places. It also encodes a moral dimension that connotes having endured the oppression and persecution of Babylon and (emblematic of the Nyahbinghi ethos) having resolutely "refused to bow" to the force of the system. It means having come through trials and tribulations with one's faith and dignity intact. In the contemporary Rastafari context, elders who were grounded in these places frequently reference them as an indication of the fact that they are "coming from far" to contrast themselves invidiously with younger individuals who are sometimes seen as "hurry-come-up Rastas". All of these phrases are idiomatic expressions, the meanings of which become clear through grounding with the brethren.

32. In this regard, we should acknowledge that there are obviously multiple registers or "versions" of grounding within Rastafari that reflect not only organizational differences (for instance, a Nyahbinghi grounding, Boboshanti grounding, Twelve Tribes grounding, an Unaffiliated grounding), but also generational as well as locational (rural versus urban) differences.

33. For those who are oriented to the ethnohistory of the movement, this example is potentially revealing on several levels. It suggests the fact that elders may selectively disclose or conceal information about their own ritual biographies. This kind of "silencing" or selective disclosure may reflect the changing and emergent ideological dynamics of Rastafari as well as the high degree of individualism that exists within the movement – its collective principles notwithstanding. At the same time, the "screening off" of other

influential contacts may, as is well known by fieldworkers, reflect pragmatic considerations. Not the least of these is that researchers are associated with resources that one or more elders prefer to monopolize within their own circle of influence.

34. Both the iterative and generative genres uphold the interpretive paradigm of Zion–Babylon, but only the generative form is capable of producing new meanings and understandings (see Homiak 1999; Yawney 1985a; 1985b).

35. If Planno was the most influential Rastafari during the second half of the movement's development, Boanerges warrants recognition as the elder most responsible for the international spread of the Nyahbinghi Order.

36. This is clearly the case within the Jamaican-based Rastafari movement. The Ethio-Africa Diasporic Millennium Council would be an illustrative example.

37. Yawney was also well aware that her grounding could, and did, elicit an opposite reaction among some Rastafari, especially in well-established communities with their own spokespersons. Yawney and I have found it to be the case that our "penetration" into the inner sanctums of Rastafari can be deeply resented by younger brethren and sistren who aspire to positions of influence within the movement. As white non-Rastafari knowledgeable about the culture, we can be seen as interlopers and, we assume, at times resented not only for the close relationships we have or have had with some of the movement's historic figures but because we may be perceived as being in positions to compete with them in representing Rastafari institutionally. This, for example, was characteristic of some of the agonistic politics that developed around the Smithsonian's *Discovering Rastafari* exhibition in 2007. This kind of tension exists among the Rastafari themselves.

38. In this, she was a prolific letter writer – doing this in longhand – and routinely sharing photographs and memorabilia that were meaningful to the relationship. The archive of papers and such resources that she deposited with the Smithsonian attests to her dedication and commitment in this regard.

39. This almost always facilitated her entry into a community. In the global sphere, this was important because if the range of heterogeneity within Rastafari was extensive in Jamaica, its range of expression was even more complex within the process of globalization. The access that grounding provided Yawney enabled her to acquire a better sense of this heterogeneity and local histories of Rastafari struggle.

40. The annual Caribbean Studies Association meeting this year featured a Rastafari panel chaired by Ras Leahcim Semaj and the scheduled screening of

the film *Rastafari Voices* by Elliott Leib, a white American graduate student in anthropology, and his wife Rene Romano. Despite great interest on the part of the Kittian Rastafari community to view and discuss the film, Semaj declined to screen it. In our discussions about the event, Carole felt that Semaj, joined by several non-Rasta Jamaican scholars, censored the film. She reiterated to me essentially what she had written to another colleague, saying that "They wanted a tourist board image of Jamaica and a certain projection of the 'modern' Rasta which wasn't forthcoming. They didn't want to have to deal with the kind of poverty, culture, and lifestyle projected in the film, or recognize it as part of 'modern' Jamaica" (letter to Klaus de Albuquerque, 19 February 1985, Papers of Carole D. Yawney, Correspondence Series, D-E, Smithsonian National Anthropological Archives).

41. Elsewhere I have argued that during the 1980s, Nyahbinghi assemblies became a site of struggle over the definition of the movement and its culture as African and its members as "Africans" as well as its traditional goal of repatriation (Homiak 1999, 104–8; see also Yawney 1999, 154–56). This followed somewhat predictably from the co-optation of Rastafari during the Manley period of the 1970s.

42. Interested readers should see the documentary film *Rastafari: Conversations about Women* by Rene Romano and Elliot Leib. Eye-in-I Filmworks, 1983.

43. One of the earliest published statements by a Rastafari woman critiquing the position of women within Rastafari is that of Maureen Rowe, published under the pseudonym "Sister Ilaloo" in the ephemera *Yard Roots* published in Southern California.

44. The *Holy Piby* was authored by the Anguillan proto-Rastafarian Shepard Robert Athlyi Rogers. Rogers, who had also been a Garveyite, published it in two versions in 1922 and 1924 in Perth Amboy, New Jersey, as the religious text for his organization, the Athlyi Constructive Gaathly, New Jersey. He later founded a branch of the Gaathly in Kimberley, South Africa, where the office of that branch was still in existence when Yawney visited in July 2000. Perhaps prophetically, it was located within sight of a Rastafari Nyahbinghi tabernacle.

45. The International Rastafari Archives Project remains an ongoing project. For the past three years I have been working with a Rastafari steering committee to enable this project as a way not only to preserve a component of Rastafari intellectual property by to generate a revenue stream for the movement.

46. MOVE is the name of an urban black activist organization started in Philadelphia during the 1970s to agitate for the fair treatment of blacks by the dominant society and particularly the criminal justice system. Today it is most closely identified with the cause and case of Mumia Abul Jamal.
47. Yawney is one of the few scholars to write about Ital livity from a combined cultural, religious and holistic health perspective (see Yawney 1985b).

References

Bammer, Angelika. 1994. Introduction. In *Displacements*, edited by Angelika Bammer. Bloomington: University of Indiana Press.

Barrett, Leonard. 1969. *The Rastafarians: A Study in Messianic Cultism in Jamaica*. Caribbean Monograph Series, no. 6. Institute of Caribbean Studies: University of Puerto Rico.

Bowen, Errol W. 1971. "Rastafarism and the New Society". *Savacou* 5: 41–50.

Burridge, Kenelm. 1969. *New Heaven, New Earth: A Study of Millenarian Activities*. Oxford: Blackwell.

Carnegie, Charles. 1999. "Garvey and the Black Transnation". *Small Axe* 5: 48–71.

Chevannes, Barry. 1976. "Repairer of the Breach: Reverend Claudius Henry and Jamaican Society". In *Ethnicity in the Americas*, edited by Frances Henry. The Hague: Mouton.

———. 1994. *Rastafari: Roots and Ideology*. New York: Syracuse University Press.

Clifford, James. 1992. "Traveling Cultures". In *Cultural Studies*, edited by Lawrence Grossberg, Cary Nelson and Paula Treichler. New York: Routledge.

Fernandez, James. 1986. "The Argument of Images and the Experience of Returning to the Whole". In *The Anthropology of Experience*, edited by Victor Turner and Edward Bruner. Chicago: University of Illinois Press.

Geertz, Clifford. 1973. "Religion as a Cultural System". In *The Interpretation of Cultures: Selected Essays by Clifford Geertz*. New York: Harper Colophon Books.

Gilroy, Paul. 1993. *The Black Atlantic: Modernity and Double Consciousness*. Cambridge: Harvard University Press.

Herzfeld, Michael. 1997. *Cultural Intimacy: The Social Politics of the Nation-State*. London: Routledge.

Hill, Robert. 1981. "Dread History: Leonard P. Howell and Millenarian Visions in Early Rastafari Religions in Jamaica". *Epoché: Journal of the History of Religions at UCLA* 9: 30–71.

Hoenisch, Michael. 1988. "Symbolic Politics: Perceptions of the Early Rastafari Movement". *Massachusetts Review* 29 (3): 482–548.

Homiak, John. 1995. "Dub History: Soundings on Rastafari Livity and Language". In *Rastafari and Other African-Caribbean Worldviews*, edited by Barry Chevannes. London: Macmillan.

———. 1996. "Review of Rastafari and Jamaican Society, 1930–1990, Frank Jan van Dijk". *New West Indies Guide* 45: 786–89.

———. 1999. "Movement of Jah People: From Soundscape to Mediascape". In *Religion, Diaspora and Cultural Identity: A Reader in the Anglophone Caribbean*, edited by John Pulis. Toronto: Gordon Breach Publishers.

Jah Bones. 1985. *One Love*. London: Voice of Rasta Publishing House.

Kitzinger, Sheila. 1969. "Protest and Mysticism: The Rastafari Cult of Jamaica". *Journal for the Scientific Study of Religion* 8: 240–61.

Lewis, Rupert. 1998. *Walter Rodney's Intellectual and Political Thought*. Kingston: University of the West Indies Press.

Littlejohn, Maureen, Maureen Sheridan and Rosie Levine. N.d. "Jamaica: Rastas, Reggae, Reefer". *Graffiti* 3 (1): 30–35.

Murrell, Samuel N., William D. Spencer and Adrian A. McFarlane, eds. 1998. *Chanting Down Babylon: The Rastafari Reader*. Philadelphia: Temple University Press.

Nettleford, Rex. 1972. *Identity, Race and Protest in Jamaica*. New York: William Morrow.

Owens, Joseph. 1976. *The Rastafarians of Jamaica*. Kingston: Sangsters.

Patterson, Orlando. 1964. "Ras Tafari: Cult of Outcasts". *New Society* 4 (3): 15–17.

Pollard, Velma. 1994. *Dread Talk: The Language of Rastafari*. Kingston: Canoe Press UWI.

Polier, Nichole and William Roseberry. 1989. "Triste Tropes: Postmodern Anthropologists Encounter the Other and Discover Themselves". *Economy and Society* 18: 245–64.

Post, Ken. 1981. *Strike the Iron: A Colony at War: Jamaica 1939–1945*. Vol. 1. Atlantic Highlands, NJ: Humanities Press.

Rappaport, Roy A. 1979. *Ecology, Meaning and Religion*. Berkeley: North Atlantic Books.

———. 1988. "Evolutionary Ecology and the Human Condition". 12th International Congress of Anthropological and Ethnological Sciences. Zagreb, Yugoslavia.

Rowe, Maureen. 1985. *The Women in Rastafari*. Caribbean Quarterly monograph. Kingston: University of the West Indies.

Simpson, George E. 1955a. "Political Cultism in West Kingston, Jamaica". *Social and Economic Studies* 4 (2): 133–49.

———. 1955b. "The Ras Tafari Movement in Jamaica: A Study of Race and Class Conflict". *Social Forces* 34 (2): 167–70.

Smith, M.G., Roy Augier, Rex Nettleford. 1960. *Report on the Rastafari Movement in Kingston, Jamaica*. Kingston: Institute of Social and Economic Studies.

Sister Ilaloo (pseudonym for Maureen Rowe). 1981. "Rastawoman as Equal!" *Yard Roots* (April/May): 5–7.

Taggart, James M., and Alan Sandstrom. 2011. "Introduction to 'Long Term Fieldwork'". *Anthropology and Humanism* 36 (1): 1–6.

Yawney, Carole D. 1972. "Herbs and the Chalice: The Symbolic Life of the Children of Slaves in Jamaica". ADARF Substudy no. 522. McGill University. Montreal, Canada.

———. 1976. "Remnants of all Nations: Rastafarian Attitudes to Race and Nationality". In *Ethnicity in the Americas*, edited by Frances Henry. The Hague: Mouton.

———. 1978. "Lions in Babylon: The Rastafarians of Jamaica as a Visionary Movement". PhD diss. McGill University, Montreal, Canada.

———. 1979. "Dread Wasteland: Rastafarian Ritual in West Kingston, Jamaica". In *Ritual, Symbolism, and Ceremonialism in the Americas: Studies in Symbolic Anthropology*. Occasional Publications in Anthropology, Ethnology series no. 33, edited by Ross Crumrine, 148–79. Greeley, CO: Museum of Anthropology, University of Northern Colorado.

———. 1981. "Rastafarians in Jamaica Perspective". *Rikka* 6 (1): 42–56.

———. 1983a. "To Grow a Daughter". In *Feminism in Canada*, edited by Angela Miles and G. Finn, 119–44. Montreal: Black Rose Books.

———. 1983b. "Rastafarian Sistren by the Rivers of Babylon". *Canadian Women Studies Journal* 5 (2): 73–75.

———. 1984. "Who Killed Bob Marley?" *Canadian Forum*, December, 29–31.

———. 1985a. "Don't Vex Then Pray: The Methodology of Initiation Fifteen Years Later". Paper presented at the Qualitative Research Conference, University of Waterloo, Canada.

———. 1985b. "Strictly Ital: Rastafari Livity and Holistic Health". Paper presented at the Ninth Annual Meetings of the Society for Caribbean Studies, Hertfordshire, UK.

———. 1986. "Moving with the Dawtas of Rastafari: From Myth to Reality". In *El Caribe y America Latina*, edited by Ulrich Fleishmann and I. Phaf. Frankfurt/Main: Verlag Klaus Dieter Vervuert.

———. 1992. "Rasta Mek a Trod: Symbolic Ambiguity in a Globalizing Religion". In *Alternative Cultures in the Caribbean*, edited by Ulrich Fleishmann and T. Bremer. Frankfurt/Main: Verlag Klaus Dieter Vervuert.

———. 1995. "Tell Out King Rastafari Doctrine Around the Whole World: Rastafari in Global Perspective". In *The Reordering of Culture: Latin America, the Caribbean, and Canada*, edited by A. Ruprecht and C. Taiana. Ottawa: Carlton University Press.

———. 1999. "Only Visitors Here: Representing Rastafari into the 21st Century". In *Religion, Diaspora, and Cultural Identity*, edited by John Pulis. Amsterdam: Gordon and Breach.

———. 2001. (with John Homiak). "Rastafari" and "Rastafari in Global Context". Gener-

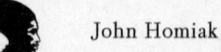

al and specific entries. In *Encyclopedia of African and African-American Religions*, edited by Stephen Glazier, 256–71. New York: Routledge.

———. 2002. "Exodus: Rastafari, Repartiation and the African Renaissance." In *A United States of Africa?*, edited by Eddy Maloka, 133–85. Pretoria: African Institute of South Africa.

———. 2004. (with John Homiak). "Rastafari" general entry. In *Encyclopedia of Religious Rites, Rituals and Festivals*, edited by F. Salamone. New York: Routledge.

Yawney, Carole, and John P. Homiak. 1999. "The Kingston–Cape Town Connection: Rastafari in South Africa". Paper presented at the Caribbean Studies Association Annual Meetings, Panama City, Panama.

Chapter 5

The Call of the Rastafari

Barry Chevannes

Good evening brothers and sisters.

Let me echo Arthur[1] that this is an extraordinary conference. I've not been to a conference quite like this before, and I've been to many. But it is all due to one man who conceptualized and pulled together a team to execute this fantastic project; who persuaded (though he didn't have to persuade too hard) the university to back this project. I don't recall that Arthur mentioned the vice chancellor in the thank-yous, but the vice chancellor contributed significantly to the project as well – not just our principal. That man, that person, is Jahlani Niaah. I'm asking you to stand and give Jahlani a standing ovation.

I'm very proud of the fact that Jahlani was my student, but now I am his student. I am learning from Jahlani to think outside the box, to always retain a zone of humility, and to find harmony in the midst of discord. It's a quality I noted Jahlani had and used when it came time to mark exam papers. Some terrible – the most terrible paper – that the student writes, and Jahlani would say: "but professor", and he gives a little angle that finds a grain of goodness and fact and possibilities within that paper – that's an extraordinary talent.

Well, I'm here not so much to deliver a closing speech, but, like Professor Augier, to *reason*. I was commenting to Arthur before the start of the conference that, in all my years of encounters with the Rastafari, I have listened. From the time I met Bongo Shephan in the 1970s, I have *listened* and interpreted and written. This is the first time I am attempting to reason; to bring ideas of my own that are outside of the beaten track in very much the same spirit as Sir Roy Augier, our keynote speaker.

So, let me begin this reasoning with reference to an interview that I gave Donisha Prendergast, Bob Marley's granddaughter, a couple of days ago. She asked me, "What would I say to her in her search for Rastafari?" I reflected and said, "You must connect to your roots. It should not be that you 'search' for Rastafari without knowing where Rastafari is coming from. As a young, bright, intellectual artist coming up in the movement, you need to appreciate and to connect with the heritage that those who have gone before have bequeathed as a legacy."

And, so, my brothers and sisters let us end this conference as we started it. Sir Roy Augier called for a minute's silence to remember Rex Nettleford and Mortimo Planno. Let us connect to the heritage that has brought us here by standing and observing a minute's silence for Robert Hines who built the largest organization of Rastafari in the city of Kingston in the 1930s and 1940s, but who died an obscure pauper's death in a hospital. Let us observe a minute's silence for Watto – Bongo Watto – founding member of the Youth Black Faith that institutionalized the dreadlocks that are now worn by so many people. Let us observe a minute's silence for Ras I – Ris I am and the Angelic Hosts of the East – who brought forth the Ital tradition of Rastafari. Let us observe a minute's silence for Bongo Purru and Bongo Time and all the other leaders who institutionalized the ritual order of the Nyahbinghi. Let us observe a minute's silence for King Emmanuel Charles Edwards, founder of the Ethiopia Africa Black International Congress, who held steadfast to the issue of reparations long before it was picked up by anybody else. Let us observe a minute's silence for the Prophet Gad, founder of the Twelve Tribes of Israel, whose wisdom expanded the reach of the Rastafari. Let us observe a minute's silence for Sister Maureen Rowe, the first Rastafari to use her scholarship to expose the male bias within the movement. Let us observe a minute's silence in tribute to these pioneers.

Thank you.

Silence is a paradox. You can speak in silence as we have just done. But silence may also be used as a weapon: a weapon of resistance. I was speaking to Yasus Afari just before this session started, and in the course of our conversation I recounted to him an event that took place right here on this campus in the 1970s in the assembly hall when, leading up to the Commonwealth heads of government meeting, the Rastafari mansions, the black power groups, the revolutionary groups, all came and staged some kind of a rally.[2] King Emmanuel had his forces who were well disciplined, enrobed I think it was in white, and they were drumming and chanting through the time. Then the Nyahbinghi came and decided to have a counter drumming. So the assembly hall, for a moment, sounded like bedlam with two different groups of Rastafari drumming. Suddenly, in response to some imperceptible signal from King Emmanuel, they all ceased drumming and everyone took a seat together, with the one exception: King Emmanuel alone remained standing before them, his eyes steadfast in front of him. For the several hours after, as the rally proceeded, when the Nyahbinghi and others carried on and spoke and so forth, and began to heckle the speakers, there was nothing but silence from King Emmanuel. And then, nearing the end of the conference rally, they got up in order and they walked out. I thought it was one of the most beautiful expressions of the use of silence to resist.

But silence may also be used as aggression. Our people have been subjected to aggression by silence. In the years leading up to his death, Rex Nettleford was collecting data for a new book. One day when I visited him, he said, "I have the title for the book". The book was to have been called, "Engaging the Silence". I had the good fortune and opportunity to see his notes after he died. Its central theme was the silencing of the African presence in Jamaica, the Caribbean and this hemisphere.

It is for this reason that Rex was drawn to Rastafari. He knew that although silence has all these uses, when you are attacked with silence you cannot counter that aggression with silence. You have to speak. And he recognized that the greatest voice, the loudest voice, resisting the silencing of the African presence was the Rastafari. In my opinion the encounters with the Rastafari, that fortune had presented Rex with, defined his career.

Think back to the time when a very bright young man from Montego Bay, Cornwall College, came to the University of the West Indies where he began that other career in dance. That would have been in the mid-1950s. Then after he graduated he won the Rhodes scholarship and went to Oxford, to Oriel College, where he read political science, studying under a great political philosopher, Isaiah Berlin. And then he came right back to the Caribbean, to the University of the West Indies, where he took a job as resident tutor – I think, in Trinidad – then he landed here, in Mona. And all of a sudden, he found himself drawn into studying the Rastas.

He would have, just like everybody else, been aware of this group, aware of Claudius Henry, aware of what was going on because of the hysteria around the place. He would have been aware of a delegation that came to the campus. And he was summoned by Arthur Lewis, the principal, who said, "Look, you and Roy Augier, and under the leadership of Mike Smith, the anthropologist, are to do this study of the Rastafari." So in a way, an opportunity came to him. It would have been nice to interview him on this point, but no doubt he would have been aware of himself as a black man. There's no question about it, because at Cornwall College he would have been one of a very few with that complexion. Cornwall College – and Munro College – that's where the scions of the Montego Bay elite went to high school; and when we speak of elite in this country, we're also talking about colour and race.

So he would have been aware, and very much cognizant of himself as a black youth, but I don't know how he distilled that sense of being black, or what he anchored it on, but what I do know is that the experience that was provided by the Rastafari in that 1960 and 1961 encounter was to shape his thinking. How do I know? Well, first of all remember now, he studied; he was a part of the team. And several times he told me, when he was recounting and recalling his memory of those years, that Arthur Lewis would sometimes come with him into the field to meet the Rastas, and on one of those trips Arthur Lewis said to him, "We are all Rastas."

So he did the study, and then was selected by the government to be one of four members of the technical mission to Africa. That technical mission, as you know, was aborted because the government called a referendum and they had to return home. But they had visited Ghana. While in Ghana, he used the opportunity to interact with Ghanaian dancers. This led to the Ghanaian government inviting Rex to come back to help them develop a National Dance Theatre in that country. I'm saying that it's the encounter with the Rastafari that gave him the opportunity. So that was another step in his understanding of that African Presence that is shared between Ghana and the Caribbean. So, it was perfectly logical that when he wrote his first book, *Mirror, Mirror*, which came out in 1970, one of the four chapters would be devoted to the Rastafari and "the call of Africa".

The book is called *Mirror, Mirror*, taken from those well-known words from the fairytale "Snow White": "Mirror, mirror on the wall who is the fairest of them all?" And he played on that word "fairest" without saying it. Being silent about that word, he just suggested it and the obscenity of looking into the mirror and asking who is the fairest of them all when what you see is a *black* face. The point, then, is that it is impossible not to be touched by Rastafari if one is in search of an *identity* in which Africa is a central component.

How many of you heard Ama Ababio?[3] In her presentation yesterday, the question that she asked was, "How does a middle class girl develop an African consciousness?" And she described how, when not more than maybe five years old, she just had a desire to write and she wrote a journal; so, she began a journal and, on seeing a Rastaman, this little child wrote that "the Rastaman reflected the rhythms of the Earth" – five or six years old! And she described how her African consciousness then "rose from this gentle awakening, to a secret longing, to an undeniable call, to a passionate pull". A gradual, almost seamless progress – and when the opportunity came, she went off for twenty beautiful years to Zimbabwe. Lovely. That's how she found her consciousness. But it began with seeing a Rastaman, who started within her "a gentle awakening".

For Sister Bunny[4] the journey was through black power and Walter Rodney who was prevented from returning to the country because he was accused of "consorting with revolutionary forces". And who do you think were those revolutionary forces? The Rastafari. These were the Rastafari in the communities of what we now call the "inner city" – Kingston. He engaged the Rastafari and helped Sister Bunny by pointing the way for her to experience the wisdom of Gad and to find her consciousness.

So, to most people then, to most of us, Rastafari represented that voice that engaged the silence. That broke the silence imposed on us – all of us – by racism. That was why Arthur Lewis could say "We're all Rastas", because he knew that they were our voice where, as a people, we needed a voice. We were being crushed by the silence. I don't know if you understand what that silence is. It's a silence about Africa. It's a silence about your connection to African. It's a silence about the achievements of Africa. That's what the silence is. Africa does not exist, and should not exist, in your consciousness. And it is this silencing that the Rastafari refused to accept.

So Rastafari was critical throughout the sixties and the seventies in re-awakening that consciousness of Africa, at a time when Garvey was dead and the focus was on independence; when emancipation was buried under a mountain of silence with only one voice, mourning and memorializing that burial, that fact of emancipation and that force; and that voice was Rastafari.

The Rastafari never allowed emancipation to be swept under the carpet. Let me explain what happened.

Independence was on 6 August 1962. Emancipation was on 1 August 1838. Between 1838 and 1961 Emancipation Day was celebrated as a holiday. I can remember that, as a schoolboy, Emancipation Day, 1 August, was a holiday. In the communities people would put on shows, concerts, to celebrate this particular day. And what our founding fathers, in their "wisdom", decided to do was to put independence above emancipation; to bury emancipation by collapsing 1 August into 6 August and celebrating independence: "You don't need no emancipation anymore because you're now free, you are now independent." But the Rastafari in their wisdom – so you had two kinds of wisdom: you had "founding father" wisdom and you had Rastafari wisdom – never once forgot about emancipation, never once allowed emancipation to go unnoticed. The Nyahbinghi Order ritualized emancipation with a *binghi* – 1 August was one of several key dates on their calendar, along with 2 November, the coronation of His Imperial Majesty, and 17 August, the birthday of Marcus Garvey.

So that, later on now in the 1990s, when conscious people began to reflect that this "wisdom" by the founding fathers was really folly, they began to agitate for a restoration of Emancipation Day. And a group of churches led by very conscious clergymen began to stage what they called "Emancipation Lectures", which was very good; then other churches began to proclaim "Emancipation Vigils" and so forth, so that the government of the day was forced to set up a commission to examine the question. Who you think led that commission? Rex Nettleford. The result was a recommendation that was accepted by the government to restore Emancipation Day.

So, what then do you think Arthur Lewis meant when he said, "We are all Rastas"? What could he have meant? I believe that we can find the answer to this if we recall what Sir Roy Augier said about the conception of Africa when he delivered his keynote address. There are two conceptions of Africa: there is Africa as geography, as place, and there is Africa as history, as *roots*. Lewis, he said, knew that Africa as geography would present insurmountable problems of cultural identity derived from the historic break. But the discovery of Africa as roots, the Africa of culture and of presence, would, he believed, help the Rastafari to grasp the idea of making Jamaica home; in truth, of finding Africa in Jamaica. Naturally, this offended many of the Rastafari who listened with keen attentiveness. But it's to his credit that Sir Roy broke the silence of the non-Rastafari surrounding that central demand by the Rastafari of repatriation.

But his speech was, as it turned out, a real keynote speech, in that as the conference developed you could see that it set a tone. So it's not surprising, then, that a tension could be felt from time to time throughout these remarkable days. Why are they remarkable? They're remarkable because, for the first time, you have a mix of participants which include Rastafari scholars on the one hand and non-Rastafari scholars on the other hand. So, this conference for the last three days has been a coming together of two different perspectives. One perspective comes from within, the other from without. One comes with faith, the other without faith. But this is not a binary. It's not a binary because coming without faith is not the opposite of coming with faith. That is what Jake [Homiak], in his presentation, showed in the case of "Goldilocks" – Sister Carole Yawney. Kumi [Mortimo Planno], if you remember the presentation, put Carole through tests before accepting her into his circle and into his mind. Carole became committed to all that Kumi stood for, and that commitment, Jake said, showed itself by her linking Kumi with the international community wherever she went. That was *her* way of fulfilling that commitment. So I'm saying that the fact there are these two perspectives doesn't mean that this conference is a coming together of binary opposites. There are no opposites here at this conference, but there is tension. And in the tone set by Sir Roy, we should not be silent about these issues. I believe that this is the place and time to raise them.

In his presentation, Ras I Vi characterized the Musgrave award[5] – an award given by the Institute of Jamaica to individuals who have excelled in the areas of literature, science and the arts – as hypocritical.[6] Until the University of the West Indies was founded in 1948 [University College then], the Institute of Jamaica was the place where intellectuals would go to get books to read and so on, because one of the first things that it did was to set up a library – and as it grew it came to have museums and so forth. The institute felt that there were some groups that they wanted to recognize, that had upheld the African presence in this country, despite denigration, despite attempts at suppressing them. These included the Maroons, the Revival religion, Kumina religion and the Rastafari religion.

Now this really was an extraordinary gesture because, if you think of what Rastafari, Revival and Kumina were up to twenty years ago, you would understand what a marvellous triumph it was for the assertion of the African presence in the country that these three groups – that had been denigrated, humiliated, whose leaders had been imprisoned or confined to asylums – would be awarded the highest recognition this institution could give, the special gold medal. Well Ras I Vi called it hypocritical because the Rastafari generally conflate institutions like that with the government. It's true that the government funds the institute, but the institute is an autonomous body, and it recognized the important role that these religions have played in upholding the African Presence and in giving the country a sense of identity that links us across the Atlantic to another space and another time.

But you could feel the tension when my good friend, and I hope he would agree that we are good friends, Yasus Afari spoke. I was not in the hall at the start of Yasus's presentation, but when I came in I connected with what he was saying about the CXC examinations.[7] He was making the point that in CXC, "the material [on Rastafari] on which the syllabus is based was written by people like Barry Chevannes and Rex Nettleford – all honour to them, but Rasta write too". Then later he said, "we don't need them to validate us", and in the course of his speech, he used the word, without calling any names "academic Rasta". He went on to use a very interesting image of an organism feeding on and assimilating another organism. You don't have to be a rocket scientist to decipher what he is saying. What he's saying is that the university is like a parasite on Rasta, using it to subvert Rasta by assimilation; or, if that is not what is being done, it could possibly happen.

So those are two examples of what I'm talking about when I speak of a tension that is present in this conference. Now you have tension that can be unproductive; the result of such tension is a trip to the psychiatrist. But tension can be good *if* it is the tension that accompanies growth, because growth produces tension. I think what Jake didn't say in his presentation was that he too – and I know this because Jake and I have been good friends and associates over the years – has been tested and criticized by the Rastafari. But he said, and I'm quoting you Jake, because I wrote it down, "Whether you like it or not, we are part of the struggle." In other words, despite the tension, we understand, and we have been taking a bashing because no matter what we do, we're "not Rasta" and are viewed with suspicion.

So the question is, what is the role of non-Rastafari scholars like Jake or myself? What is the role of the Smithsonian Institution? What is the role of this university, the University of the West Indies? You all remember that when Sir Roy mentioned that some Rastafaris used to invert "UC"[8] and call it "U-Blind", there was one heckler in the audience who said, "Still blind!" Now, brothers and sisters, this may appear funny, but it is quite interesting, because this was the same "UC" to which the brethren appealed. In other words, Arthur Lewis didn't rush out to say, "What can we do to help you?" *They* came, they visited the campus and requested that Arthur Lewis assist them, and when he assisted them, they say, "you blind, U-Blind".

A colleague of mine made a very interesting observation to me yesterday, of which I hadn't thought of before, which is that our Rastafari brothers do not deride UTech (the University of Technology), they do not deride the Northern Caribbean University. Why? I said "Ah! Because we engage." We are the only university which has had a relationship with the Rastafari over the years, beginning with the university report, then with the kinds of relationship that Rex established with the Rastafari, and with the work that I have done. Jahlani referred to Mortimo Planno, for example and the residency of Mortimo Planno at the university. It was the setting up of that *Folk Filosofi* programme at the university that brought students into contact with those men and women whose wisdom you don't find in books because they are not writers; but that doesn't mean that their wisdom is any less valid, valuable and insightful. So Kumi became the first *folk filosofer*. Bongo Jerry became the second *folk filosofer*. Mutabaruka became the third *folk filosofer*. The last two held tenure at the university for up to a year, and Kumi, as you know, stayed on for much longer because his was a special case. This is the university that seeks to accommodate, as much as it can, Rasta; but still some Rastafari delight in saying that the university is blind – "UC"/"U-Blind".

Now, brothers and sisters, this is a tension. I mention it because of the extraordinary peculiarities of this conference. At most conferences, everybody is pretty like-minded – they belong to the same discipline, and if they have differences, it's differences of theory and schools of thought, and so forth; that is known to breed tension too, but not of this kind. For this conference to have come to such a glorious end, despite, or in spite of, or perhaps because of, this tension, is extraordinary, and that is what has made it *unique*.

I do not believe that this tension between fellow strugglers – and I think I have to say "fellow strugglers" because, using Jake's words, "*Whether you like it or not,* we are a part of the struggle" – is going to go away soon. The root of it, the reason I think it won't go away soon, may be found in that keynote speech by Sir Roy: the driving motivation behind repatriation is the irreconcilability of the Rastafari with Jamaica. The issue comes down to "Africa as geography" versus "Africa as roots". I believe that as long as the choice is for "Africa as geography", then all who stand for Jamaica, or, for that contradiction we call the "West Indies", will face obstacles. No matter how helpful you are, no matter how closely aligned, no matter how brethren will embrace you, if you are not "for repatriation" then that is going to be the root of this tension that will forever exist between fellow strugglers.

But if the choice is "Africa as roots", then it becomes possible to say what Claudius Henry said to his followers: that the emperor told him that Africa is already in Jamaica so there is no need to return. This was, of course,

Barry Chevannes

after Henry had come out of prison. Then, people like myself and Rex, who excavate and assert the centrality of the African Presence in Jamaica and the rest of the Caribbean can be embraced as living in the same house, if living in different mansions. We need not be silent on this matter. And I think that the movement itself has to confront some of these issues. What of those who repatriate and then return? Why did they not stay? Was the pull of "Africa as roots" stronger than the whole of "Africa as place"? These are issues that the Rastafari community has to face.

And then there is also the meaning of repatriation. Is simply "going back", in any fashion or form, "repatriation"? Is Shashamane really repatriation – where you find your own money, you book your own passage and you go and establish a settlement and try to eke out a development? Repatriation should have an element of justice. Our ancestors who were taken are due that. Their descendants are due recompense for this injustice, and they should be allowed the choice of repatriation. Where is the justice, if we find our own resources, as Twelve Tribes have so admirably done, to leave Babylon and go back? Where is the justice in that? Have you, in doing so, absolved the perpetrator? Let him go free? These are issues that the movement should confront and not be silent about.

And then there is the global spread. This conference is a magnificent exhibition of the global reach of the Rastafari movement. I like the way that Ras Sela put it.[9] He said, "Rastafari is a constant becoming." I have found that a dynamic way of imagining what Rastafari is about. To Ras Cela it's not a Jamaican thing. It's interesting: the Jamaican Rastafari see Rastafari as originating in Jamaica, and I think most scholars do too. But here is a Panamanian, rooted and living in Panama, finding a sense of home in Rastafari; having to justify Rastafari to himself and to his community, he sees it coming out of Africa through Jamaica. That is the origin: the origin isn't Jamaica but Africa – Rastafari is only rooted through Jamaica. In other words, as a Panamanian thinker, he is trying to make Rastafari in Panama, Panamanian. Another case in point arises in looking at how Rastafari is rooted among the Maori. What do the Maori think? According to Ian Boxhill, the Maori are not thinking of repatriation to Africa. So I'm saying that, in the global reach of Rastafari, these are issues which have to be taken into account. Amaha Selassie's paper spoke about the universalizing of Rastafari philosophy through the teachings and outlook of His Imperial Majesty.[10] He sees the unification of the movement as stemming from the common thread of the belief in the divinity of King Rastafari. But, then, what of repatriation?

Another issue which clearly is a source of tension within the movement itself is what was expressed by Brother Tyehimba Salandy from Trinidad.[11] He was very bold, because he said that he hadn't seen at this conference any confronting of issues like patriarchy or (and I found this one interesting) the social and racial demarcations that place some Ras above other Ras. In other words, if you are a brown-skinned Rasta, you hold a higher status than a black-skinned Rasta. Or if you are a middle-class Rasta, you are of a higher standing than a working-class Rasta. "It is not enough", he said, "to call a woman an Empress, then turn around and dictate to her what she is to wear". These are issues that the movement has to deal with.

Finally, reggae music gave birth to and nurtured the interest in Rastafari. In so many countries in the world, Rastafari was carried on the wings of reggae music. This is clear in Mexico, this is clear in Brazil and elsewhere. The question I leave with you, my Rastafari brothers and sisters, is what is going to sustain and make the movement grow? The music clearly can't. It may have ushered in the interest but, to use Ama Ababayo's image, "a gentle awakening" leading to a sustained interest and eventually a passionate pull can only take place through the instrumentality of other events, other processes, which leads me then to my conclusion.

I do think the moment is ripe, Brother I Vi,[12] for a truly global conference – a reasoning of Rastafari by the Rastafari. There needs to be a conference, not of Rastafari studies, not by Rastafari scholars – meaning scholars of Rastafari – but by adherents of Rastafari. Every country of the world should be represented. You should have representation from among the Maori, from among the Japanese, from Italy, from Brazil, from Chile, from Cuba, from Canada, from the United States, from France, from the United Kingdom, from South Africa, because all over the world there are communities of Rastafari.

But what would be the purpose, apart from celebrating the diversity of Rastafari? It would be a reasoning to find common ground, a unity in the diversity. A very interesting paper was delivered yesterday by young Rosina Casserly.[13] She said, "I argue that the lack of uniformity in Rasta is not fatal to the Rastafari purpose of taking theories and policies of freedom to the world, but that it is the unique equipment to relieve this mandate. In fact, it is precisely because Rastafari's critical method shifts convention so radically, and is defined by the relentless, dialogical and constantly self-critical search for truth that it gives the world a New Faculty of Interpretation." She pays tribute, of course, to her teacher, Dr Jahlani Niaah, who argues that Rastafari represents this new faculty of interpretation. But, as the saying goes, "A child shall lead them" – the elderly and the experienced can learn from the young. Here's a young woman, a young student, making a forceful argument that the strength of Rastafari lies *in its diversity*.

So the celebration of that diversity would be an important step in strengthening the movement. This is not another Council of Nicaea – that was dangerous; what that did was to divide Christianity by setting up articles of faith that if you departed from you were branded a heretic. In Rasta, to preserve your strength, it would appear that Rosina is quite right. It is the diversity that must be maintained and embraced. But, let me end by quoting another "child", Donisha. I began this reasoning by referencing Donisha; let me close by referencing her. I'm quoting from what she said when she introduced the film yesterday:[14] "The truth is, mi doh know the truth. So mi have to keep searching." That to me was the sound bite of the conference. That is what I do humbly believe, Bongo Shephan, is the call of the Rastafari.

Acknowledgements

This chapter was originally presented as the closing address of the inaugural Rastafari Studies Conference in 2010.

Notes

1. This is a reference to Arthur Newland, a colleague of Chevannes and the chair of the closing session at which Chevannes provided this address.
2. Chevannes here refers to a Rastafari "rally" to suggest a type of organized protest presence during a Commonwealth Heads of Government conference, as a show of force, disruption and resistance to the official governments of the region by members of the movement and other Black Power advocates.
3. She presented the conference paper entitled "Reflections on Life in Zimbabwe (1982–2002)" on 19 August 2010.
4. This is a reference to Angela Heron, who was a student at the UWI during the Rodney Riots in 1968.
5. The award is named after Anthony Musgrave, the governor of Jamaica who was instrumental in founding the Institute of Jamaica in 1879; the institute's

The Call of the Rastafari

mandate is the promotion of literature, science and the arts. The award takes the form of bronze, silver and gold medals.

6. These comments were made during his presentation at the 2010 Rastafari studies conference entitled "Family Matters: The Creed of Rastafari".
7. CXC is short for Caribbean Examination Council, the body that certifies high school graduates.
8. The abbreviation for the University College of the West Indies, as it was called at the time (being a college of the Universityof London) until it received its charter and became University of the West Indies.
9. He chaired the conference workshop, "Report on Ethiopia" (19 August 2010).
10. This conference presentation was "Continuing the Legacy of His Imperial Majesty Emperor Haile Selassie I (18 August 2010).
11. His conference presentation was entitled "The Rasta Movement: African Caribbean Worldviews and Resistance in the Era of Globalisation" (19 August 2010).
12. Ras I Vi was one of the key spokespersons for the Nyahbinghi House and in his address he raised the need for Rastafari to become more responsible.
13. The title of her paper was " 'Hue Man Inity': Ras-Ta-Fari and Global Liberation qua Afrika", presented 19 August 2010.
14. She, along with Barbara Blake Hannah, introduced the section of the conference entitled "In Tribute to Media" (17 August 2010).

Reference

Nettleford, Rex. 1970. *Mirror, Mirror: Identity, Race and Protest in Jamaica*. Kingston: Collins and Sangster.

Contributors

Jahlani Niaah is Lecturer in Cultural and Rastafari Studies, Institute for Caribbean Studies, University of the West Indies, Mona, where he also coordinates the Rastafari Studies Unit.
Erin MacLeod teaches at Vanier College in Montreal, Canada, and has also served as a postdoctoral fellow at the University of the West Indies, Mona. Her book on Ethiopians and Rastafari is forthcoming from NYU Press.
Roy Augier is Professor Emeritus of History, University of the West Indies, Mona, and has served with distinction both as a teacher and administrator at the University of the West Indies, Mona since 1954.
Barry Chevannes was Professor of Social Anthropology, former head of the Department of Sociology, Social Work and Psychology and the former dean of the Faculty of Social Science at the University of the West Indies, Mona, and an authoritative voice on the Rastafari movement.
John Homiak is a cultural anthropologist and a long-term ethnographer of Rastafari who, along with his research partner, the late Professor Carole D. Yawney, has focused on the history and globalization of the movement.
Rex Nettleford was Professor of Cultural Studies and Vice Chancellor Emeritus, University of the West Indies, and founder, artistic director and prinicpal choreographer of the National Dance Theatre Company of Jamaica.
Mortimo Planno was a Dreadlocks leader/teacher, cum Rastafari plenipotentiary. He was the first Jamaican dreadlock Rastafari to be officially engaged by the government of Jamaica, participating in two of three "Back to Africa" missions. Between 1961 and 1971 Planno was one of the key influential teachers in West Kingston, his yard at Fifth Street in Trench Town attracting local and international visitors seeking knowledge of Rastafari as well as reggae music. He assumed a one-year fellowship at the University of the West Indies in 1998, and in 2000 Planno returned to the university until his death in 2006.

www.ingramcontent.com/pod-product-compliance
Lightning Source LLC
Chambersburg PA
CBHW020805160426
43192CB00006B/450

9 789766 404093